Ja

PSEUDONYMS OF CHRIST IN THE MODERN NOVEL

PSEUDONYMS
OF
CHRIST
IN
THE
MODERN
NOVEL

Motifs and Methods
by
Edwin M. Moseley

MANUFACTURED IN THE UNITED STATES OF AMERICA
BOOK CRAFTSMEN ASSOCIATES, INC., NEW YORK

FOR
Catharine, Stephen, and Quentin

A Preface: After the Fact

WHEN I reexamine the essays which follow, I find that they have treated some things which I intended from the beginning and some other things that evolved in the course of my work. Originally I was interested in the current religious climate of literary creation and literary criticism. It seemed to me that suddenly many readers, including myself, were discovering religious patterns, conscious and unconscious, in the fiction of the last century and that, in line with this discovery, the books of many recent writers revealed a concern with religious themes and a pertinent use of religious symbolism. I was particularly interested in the recurrence of the Christ archetype in a series of novels quite dissimilar on the surface but basically alike in what they had to say.

As I deliberately considered these similarities which I had more or less intuitively discovered, I came to realize that the important point was not so much how these works were alike as how they were different while being alike. My main interest became the variations on the

same pattern, variations which I soon related to the
changing climate of opinion almost from decade to decade. It is amazing that attitudes and emphases change so
rapidly in our time! That this can be so was brought
home forcefully to me by William Appleman Williams'
article in *The Nation* of November 2, 1957: "The
American Century: 1941-1947."

The books which I have utilized in my study are, in
my opinion, highly effective novels, but I have chosen
them in part because they are representatives, respectively, of particular facets of the modern climate. The
first three: Conrad's *Lord Jim* (1900), Dostoyevsky's
Crime and Punishment (1866), and Turgenev's *Fathers
and Sons* (1861), all pre-World War I novels and indeed nineteenth-century ones, express orthodox religious
attitudes on the part of the authors and tend to handle
the Christ figure traditionally and respectfully. They are
all keenly aware of the "scientific" rejection of religion
in their time and, if the books are approached in part as
problem novels, may indeed be primarily concerned with
criticizing the new scientism. These books, actually strikingly different from each other in method, take a last
stand on behalf of what I define as the essential values of
any religion. I feel that in more literary terms these writers believe in and utilize the mode of tragedy, which I
have called the most religious of literary forms.

The next three books—Lawrence's *Sons and Lovers*
(1913), Remarque's *All Quiet on the Western Front*
(1929), and Fitzgerald's *The Great Gatsby* (1925)—are
in essence post-World War I novels or at least in fact
post-Victorian ones. It is too easy to say they reject
orthodox morality, for that is not entirely so or even altogether pertinent. But the new naturalism, psychological

and sociological, has had its impact on these books. The desperate pleas of Conrad, Dostoyevsky, and Turgenev to maintain faith have hardly been heeded. The nostalgia for a traditional religious pattern or the irony of its absence or the perversion and mock-use of such—in summary, the impossibility of an orthodox pattern—are significant for the 1920's in large part because only ten years before such a pattern might have been used unquestioningly and positively.

Faulkner's *Light in August* (1932), Forster's *Passage to India* (1924), Steinbeck's *Grapes of Wrath* (1939), Silone's *Bread and Wine* (1936), Malraux' *Man's Fate* (1933), and Koestler's *Darkness at Noon* (1941), which form the next group, are held together by the tenuous classification of being socially-conscious novels. They are all so much more than that; but again, in contrast to the group from the 1920's, they deal on the literal level, which demands attention first, with social problems. As to solutions for these problems, they run the gamut from the individualism of Forster, to the socialism of Steinbeck, to the synthesis of these in, say, Silone. In themselves they form a history of social attitudes from the 1920's to the 1940's and remind us of the primary concern with solving material problems in the 1930's. The Christ pattern in these books is manifold and relevant. The Christ of social novels must be concerned with the here, not the hereafter, and this particular kind of seriousness makes tragedy a difficult mode.

The last two books I discuss are *The Stranger* by Camus (1942) and *The Old Man and the Sea* by Hemingway (1953). (I might emphasize that throughout my studies Hemingway has been a kind of correlative for the other writers and that, along the way, I have talked

about many pieces by him.) Both of these works suggest
a recrudescence of the tragic mode in recent years, paradoxically both through the mock religious imagery of
atheistic existentialism and through the positive analogues
of Greek tragedy and the Judeo-Christian Scriptures.
Here is where we are *now*, and one of my concerns has
been to suggest *how* and *why* we have run the full
cycle back to orthodoxy in religion and orthodoxy in
literature. I have no answers, merely suggestions that I
hope will provoke the reader to find the answers for
himself.

This summary of my chapters would imply that my
study is primarily social and intellectual history. In part,
yes, but primarily, no. I have mentioned the books in the
order in which I considered them, and the reader has
probably noticed its deviations from strict chronology.
The order was determined in part by the history of ideas
but in part too by the methods of the writers, a kind of
history of style and mode, and in large part by the methods demanded of readers. This last factor brings one to
the evolvement of the book as an anthology of critical
methods.

If the seemingly insoluble social plight of man has
once again made the tragic mode possible for writers, it
is only natural that this same plight has made a sense of
tragic patterns possible for readers and critics. The tragic
correlative most strikingly a part of the awareness of
Western man—writer, reader, or indeed non-reader—is
the correlative of Christ or, in a broader sense, the pattern of learning through suffering as endlessly and recurrently dramatized by Christ. It does not matter whether
this pattern is approached anthropologically from pre-
and non-Christian rituals and fertility rites, psychologi-

cally via Jung or Freud and the warfare of the generations, socio-economically via Marxism, ex-Marxism, and
Christian socialism in terms of dying and revitalized societies, or metaphysically and theologically via crisis-
and-redefinition or death-and-resurrection, still the pattern will be found strikingly in the modern awareness.
An author's lack of conscious intention could not keep
the pattern out of the modern awareness even if the author tried to do so.

If my book is at all effective, the reader will learn
that critical approaches are not exclusive of each other
and that in reading a book a certain approach may be
more fruitful than another. And he may learn to read in
a way that he has not read before. I do not mean to be
presumptuous in suggesting that mine is a better way to
read, but I simply want to make clear, for better or for
worse, how we *are* tending to read *now*. In this connection, I have tried to point out the dangers and excesses of
the new mythic or religious criticism as well as its rich
and provocative results.

Acknowledgments

Catharine Fisher Moseley, my wife; John Pickering of Holt, Rinehart, and Winston; Daniel Curley of the University of Illinois; Lee Yosha of the University of Hartford; and Frederick Hetzel of the University of Pittsburgh Press have encouraged in many ways the completion of this work. Many of my students have contributed to it by listening to, discussing in, and writing for my classes in the modern novel at Washington and Jefferson College.

Sections of the chapters on Conrad and Steinbeck have been read at the annual convention of the Modern Language Association. The first chapter and parts of the chapters on Camus and Hemingway were read as a part of the University of Michigan English Department Series on Approaches to Contemporary Literature. The chapter on Fitzgerald was read before the University of Pittsburgh Graduate Humanities Club. Parts of the last chapter were included in a lecture given at the Portland (Oregon) State College Festival of Contemporary Arts.

EDWIN M. MOSELEY
Dean of the Faculty and Professor of English
Skidmore College, Saratoga Springs, New York

Contents

PSEUDONYMS OF CHRIST IN THE MODERN NOVEL

In The Beginning . . .

IN one of the great
moments of modern literature Frederic Henry, the protagonist of Hemingway's *A Farewell to Arms,* plays
billiards with the ninety-four-year-old Italian aristocrat,
Count Greffi. The two men are drinking a wine which
is "icy cold and very dry and good," qualities which
the appreciative critic might attribute to the scene itself.
Lieutenant Henry does not want to talk about the war;
he must convince himself of the impossible, that is, that
he has made a separate peace with it. He cannot talk
about his recent reading, for he has had little opportunity to read anything that is worth mentioning. He
will not talk about the soul, for he and Count Greffi
agree that they know nothing about it.

"Are you *Croyant?*" asks the Count. "At night,"
Henry replies, and the Count continues as if in a mono-
logue: "I had expected to become more devout as I
grow older but somehow I haven't. It is a great pity."
Later he reiterates that he had expected to become
devout, "But somehow it does not come." "It's too
early," Henry consoles him. "Maybe it is too late,"

Count Greffi answers. "Perhaps I have outlived my religious feeling."

Count Greffi is like the history of an age, with his
white hair and mustache and his nineteenth-century
manners. He has been a diplomat. His birthday parties
were great social events. His game of billiards is still
smoothly fluent. Earlier in the novel Catherine Barkley,
the heroine, said that she was brought up to believe that
everything had an explanation, but that the war has
shattered her illusion of order. In appearance and bearing, Count Greffi is a walking symbol of this illusion,
but his attitudes are described as brittle and he is afraid
that he will break off a finger "as one breaks a stick of
chalk." He is near the end of an era, but he contends
that he has found no beginning. Still, the essence of a
beginning is present.

"Do younger nations always win wars?" asks Lieutenant Henry. "They are apt to for a time," says the
Count. "Then what happens?" asks Henry again. "They
become older nations." Henry wisely accuses Count
Greffi of wisdom, but the Count denies wisdom and
claims "cynicism." After all, the Count may have shown
considerable insight into himself, for to end his statements here is neither religious nor wise.

The unrefined Italian enlisted men may be wiser.
They have already told Henry that only those who
suffer are wise, and Henry has found himself parodying them. "How would Our Lord have been if Peter had
rescued him in the Garden?" he asks a priest. And of the
peasants who taught him this: "The peasant has wisdom,
because he is defeated from the start. Put him in power
and see how wise he is."

Things begin to coalesce. Peasants and old nations

are wise: the innocent and the experienced, the intuitive and the sophisticated, the beginning and the end, the end and the beginning. In the quoted passages is the core of all religion and of tragedy, which is the most religious of literary genres. Lieutenant Henry can listen to these things and articulate them, but really he is not ready to live them: "It's too early." He is like Oedipus who, as a young man, confounds the Sphinx with the magical reply to the riddle, but denies his own understanding of his reply by the action that follows. His understanding can come only with experience.

Elsewhere, too, Hemingway's young protagonists have contended that they are not ready. They cannot fit the suffering of the worm into the ritual of fishing; somehow, in their systems they cannot find a place for sacrifice and suffering. They can go through all of the ritualistic forms, but their very feelings and senses tell them that they are not ready for the tragic adventure, which is the drama of religion.

The resistance to suffering is conspicuously a part of the early Hemingway code. Count Greffi's other religious truth—his first is that younger nations become older nations—is that "love . . . is a religious feeling." If Count Greffi presents his first truth cynically, he presents his second emptily. He himself is alone. Lieutenant Henry is in love, yes, but he has kept telling himself that love will bring only loss and hurt. He has listened to the warnings of Hemingway's supposedly more experienced characters, such as Lieutenant Rinaldi and the nurse Ferguson, against the dangers of emotional involvement. If Henry has yet to fit sacrifice into his scheme, he has yet to learn the essentially religious truth that the sacrifices of love are worthwhile because without love there is nothing. The choice, then, is between sacrifice and nothing. Ergo, sacrifice is everything, and that is what Henry is not prepared to accept. The literal sacrifice that he makes at the end of *A Farewell to Arms* is pathetic, not cathartic. He does not find through his loss a sense of oneness with some vastness about him.

If we attribute the lack of religious readiness of Hemingway's protagonists to literal and experiential youthfulness, what then of Count Greffi, who is ninety-four and will probably reach an even hundred years? In his polish and detachment (he has been in the diplomatic service of *both* Austria and Italy, the traditional enemies) is he guilty of a kind of Spenglerian decadence? Is he the man who has become so refined that he has ceased to be civilized, assuming that civilization implies involvement in a moral code? Or is he a phenomenon of his own century in which a belief in human reason and an ordered universe has been dissipated by a naturalistic redescription of things? To his forebears religion has always come at the end, but to him, alas, it has not. Though he can articulate the essential truths of religion, he cannot feel them. This plight is the pathetic one of the true sophisticate.

Are we merely talking about characters in a book? Yes and no. Here are the things Hemingway is capable of having his characters say and feel and do, here is the early Hemingway, and here is the climate of an entire generation of writers. A few years ago Professor John Aldridge said that it was time to talk about *After the Lost Generation,* and he was indeed right. But he did not altogether do this, for he talked primarily about new, young writers who also know nothing about the soul. Of course they are from another decade, and they have been given epigrammatic designations such as "anxious" and "beat" instead of "lost." But at their young ages the new writers are no more ready for the essential themes than the young Hemingway was. To get beyond the lost generation one must watch *it* grow out of cynicism into wisdom. I suspect that the magnificent pieces of writing, such as the true epics and unforced tragedies and unashamedly *croyant* novels, evolve from the happy coalition of the writer who is faced with death and the age which is faced with death. A writer old when an age is young may be merely nostalgic, a writer young when an age is old may be merely cynical, but a writer old when an age is old has the true wisdom. It is out of a profound sense of personal and social end that the great religions have evolved, as has the great literature which dramatized them.

The religious overtones and undertones of much of the recent serious literature, most of it written by established authors who were once too young to be religious, might make us ask: what manner of end are we experiencing? Any attempt at such social definition would be general and banal. Still, the religious climate of current creative writing and creative reading is impressive.

T. S. Eliot once spoke of the attributes of art as sincerity, skill, and significance. The last of these is the most difficult to determine without the advantage of distance, and even discovery of the first two may be as much a matter of the critic's taste and intuition as of his considered judgment. Still, we recognize that the artist *somehow* achieves the magic combination of skill and feeling, the conscious craft and the unconscious talent, the personal detail and the archetypal detail, the known and the forgotten. Any artistic coming together of these *is* magic, for skill without sincerity is as sterile as sincerity without skill is pathetic. By way perhaps of apologizing for what I am about to do in the essays which follow, I am getting around to saying that creative reading also involves a kind of magic combination of the conscious and the unconscious response. The writer who uses his symbolism with painstaking self-consciousness may turn out a stilted and unmoving book, and the reader who can recognize the symbolic pattern of, say, "ritual mime" in the structure of a book without a simultaneous emotional immersion in the interplay of detail, has somehow fed on the book without consuming it. A few years ago in an issue of the *Kenyon Review*, Mr. Philip Rahv, an editor of the *Partisan Review* since its founding, criticized with some justification the "bias toward symbolism, allegory and mythic patterning in the reading of fiction" as having a "debilitating effect on the critical mind." But what Mr. Rahv did not admit is that in our time we cannot help reading the way we read. When we have truly felt the books we read, we have always intuitively seen their meanings, but our increased religious awareness has brought us to new conscious insights, many of which fall into the category of criticism that Mr. Rahv attacks. We reread, say, an early story by Hemingway, and we are aware of things that we must have known before when we first *felt* the story, but could not have articulated. We are often ashamed at being able to articulate our feelings, but they are before us; we now read in this way, and we must be true to our *undeliberate* reading. Our new sense of religious and mythic patterns where we did not see them before is frighteningly a symptom that we sense ends so thoroughly that we have arrived at a need for beginnings.

It was not so very long ago, less than a decade to be sure, that the Douglas Bushes were attacking the Cleanth Brookses as the new critics. In the article mentioned Mr. Rahv, a kind of double new critic in that he edits one new critic journal and speaks through another, is attacking the newer critics. The new critics and the newer critics cannot help reading the way they did read and do read, and to previous readers the new way is always debilitating.

Suddenly, then, we seem ready to read in the way that I try to suggest in the pages which follow, just as the writers are all but suddenly ready to write in a way that demands this kind of reading. And a way, furthermore, that demands a rereading of their books in the past. Few writers are kind to their critics, but an example of true kindness that I recall was Thomas Mann's fine article on "The Making of 'The Magic Mountain' " in the *Atlantic Monthly* a few years ago. Having discussed the experiential, attitudinal, and literary sources of the novel and having stated his conscious literary intentions in it, Mann went on to say that in a manuscript devoted to his works Howard Nemerov had pointed out a grail pattern in the theme and imagery of *The Magic Mountain*. Mr. Mann said that he had not been aware of utilizing such a pattern, but that he had reexamined the novel along the lines that Mr. Nemerov defined, and had to admit first, "perhaps he is right" and, finally, in effect, "By God, it is there!" Mr. Nemerov could no more have helped discovering this mythic patterning than Mr. Mann could have helped using it. And, too, one wonders if Mr. Nemerov was aware of this pattern when he first read the book a while back.

I must admit that much of the religious and mythic symbolism, inverted or positive, that I see in the books which I have reexamined I did not see in my earlier readings—though in some cases I had read the books many times. I do not think that I am imposing implications: in several cases, without recognition of these, there is no definition of the total structure of the books. The psychological and social orientations of the 'twenties and the 'thirties, for example, are not replaced by the present varieties of non-determinism in all fields of thinking; they are included in it, added to it, and enriched by it. The attractiveness of a religiously-implicit redescription of things is due to our needs to articulate a more profound sense of universal values, whether or not a concern with these is an admission that the current social problems seem to the intellectual insoluble. If you will, call the concern with transcendent values *escape;* still, the concern is there, and it is widespread at the moment.

I mention below that a group of writers and scholars in the late 'thirties designated Spengler, Dewey, Turner, Beard, Veblen, Parrington, Richards, Boas, Sumner, Henry Adams, Freud, and Lenin as the twentieth-century influences on the dominant climate of opinion. With due respect to this list of dramatic and imaginative thinkers, I wonder only two decades later what names we should add to these or replace them with. What of Keynes, Toynbee, Whitehead, Niebuhr, Einstein, Sartre, Gandhi, Schweitzer, Jung—names which suggest a resurrection of secular and ecclesiastical individualism, a belief in original and ultimate good, the discovery of a transcendental oneness in diversity, a moral pattern of history, and the possibility of the exemplary life and hence a reverence for life? Are these the new heroes in the current mythology? And does even our way of reading, small matter that it is, reflect our participation in their universe?

My comments which follow will hardly please, say, the professional Jungian whose language is as metaphorical and as technical as that of his psychological and sociological antagonists. But I realize that in my recognition of similar religious awareness, conscious and unconscious, on the part of the authors whom I consider, I am dealing in part with Jung's "mythological types" or "archetypes." Perhaps more to the point, I am dealing with the peculiarly Western version of the savior-archetype in the figure of Christ, and I am dealing furthermore with topical variations of the Western version as the men-and-the-moments change. In terms of archetypes Faulkner's story "The Bear" is among other things a story of the rites of passage, of initiation of a young boy into manhood and maturity, of the process of what Jung and his disciples call "individuation," but in other terms it is also a story of individual psychological development with emphasis on the son-father relationship and it is a story of growing up in the South, fitting into what Malcolm Cowley called Faulkner's "Southern epic." As Faulkner has the father of the boy say in a discussion of Keats' "Ode on a Grecian Urn," the author has to write about *something*. The *something* is specific character and specific environment, but beyond these the author is concerned with persons and experiences true for all places and all times. We, the readers, respond to the varieties of *somethings* through which the authors imply *everything*. Again, they succeed in doing so through reaching the magical point at which they know and do not know what they are doing.

To all modern schools of criticism, the relationship of the work to the author is that of the dream to the dreamer. The assumption must be that the analyst may be able to see things in the dream which the dreamer himself cannot. Then what is left is the doctor's wish that the patient will be kind enough to say, as Mann has said, that it *is* there. The critic, to be sure, never even comes close to knowing *all*. As I say repeatedly below, the only *all* is the work itself, and I remain embarrassingly humble in the knowledge that I am abstracting parts from wholes and truly adding nothing to one's understanding of the work in question if he has *felt* it as intensely as he can.

BIBLIOGRAPHICAL NOTE:

THE NEWER CRITICISM

Philip Rahv raised his question about myth and literature in "Fiction and the Criticism of Fiction," *The Kenyon Review,* Spring, 1956, a question which has become a rhetorical one with an affirmative answer. In any case it was asked somewhat belatedly. I am of course not referring to such traditional recognitions of references to mythology as Douglas Bush's *Mythology and the Renaissance Tradition in English Poetry* (Minneapolis, 1932) and *Mythology and the Romantic Tradition in English Poetry* (Cambridge, Mass., 1937), but to such books as Suzanne K. Langer's *Philosophy in a New Key: A Study of the Symbolism of Reason, Rite, and Art* (Cambridge, Mass., 1942) and Lord Raglan's *The Hero: A Study in Tradition, Myth, and Drama* (London, 1937; New York, 1956), which cannot be considered primarily or properly works of literary criticism. Thomas Mann's *Atlantic Monthly* article on "The Making of 'The Magic Mountain'" appeared in January, 1953, but he had already collaborated interestingly with Karl Kerenyi on *Romandichtung und Mythologie* (Zurich, 1945). We need no longer talk about seeking myth as Richard Chase did in his well-known *Quest for Myth* (Baton Rouge, 1949). We know only too well that it has been *found,* willy-nilly, and found so strikingly that *Daedalus,* the journal of the American Academy of Arts and Sciences, must talk in an entire issue about the discovery ("Myth and Mythmaking," Spring, 1959). Still, some of the authors in the issue seem bothered by what they have caught hold of without, somehow, wanting to catch it.

The contest between Douglas Bush as scholar and Cleanth Brooks as new critic waxed in 1948-1949 in articles and in speeches (Mr. Bush needled the then new critics in a major address at the Modern Language Association, and Mr. Brooks answered at a University of Pittsburgh Writers' and Readers' Conference)—and it waxed in the decade before and the decade after in college English departments throughout the country. Mr. Brooks and his friends won through such subverting weapons as the freshman texts *Understanding Fiction* (New York, 1943), *Understanding Drama* (New York, 1948), and *Understanding Poetry* (New York, 1950), but only in time to be faced with a movement from explication toward the recognition of patterns vastly broader than the socially implicit ones they had rejected. My series of essays is admittedly concerned with patterns so broad as to be elusive, but the turning inward demanded by the new criticism has frequently been, if one likes, the trap toward turning outward which characterizes what I call the newer criticism.

II

Christ As Tragic Hero:

CONRAD'S
Lord Jim

WRITING in the last decade of the nineteenth century and for almost twenty-five years thereafter, Joseph Conrad was considerably bothered by the themes and techniques of the literary naturalists. They were expressing themselves on the continent and in America with self-conscious forthrightness about the complete physicality of man. In "Prince Roman" (1911) Conrad was just as explicit in his non-naturalism as Zola, Norris, Sinclair, *et al.* were inclined to be in their opposing theses. He accused "the vulgar refinement of modern thought" of being incapable of "a certain greatness of soul" and "a sincerity of feeling." To Conrad, the new thought omitted what was necessary for understanding "the august simplicity of a sentiment proceeding from the very nature of things and men." The specific sentiment that he had in mind was "patriotism," for which his protagonist, Prince Roman, had an impressive capacity. A decade later belief in sacrifice for a social cause, national or otherwise, was the concept most debunked by a young generation

brought up intellectually on naturalism or directed to
it by their experience in the First World War and the
disillusioning days that followed. In the very year of
Conrad's death, Hemingway was to depict modern
man's futile search for a soul in *The Sun Also Rises*, and
four years later he was to make in *A Farewell to Arms*
the much quoted statement: "Abstract words such as
glory, honor, courage, or hallow were obscene beside
the concrete names of villages, the numbers of roads, the
names of rivers, the numbers of regiments and the
dates."

Two separate worlds of thinking and of writing,
each sensitively aware of the other, are reflected in the
quotations from Conrad and Hemingway. To Conrad
there was an essence beyond the observable, and man
had a capacity for reaching and expressing it. Any denial
of this capacity was a "vulgar refinement." To the early
Hemingway the verbal expression of such a capacity
was mere rationalization, "obscene" in its very hypocrisy.

Still, Conrad was hardly naïve about the pretenses
of man to himself. At the beginning of the century he
had published in *Heart of Darkness* a devastating criticism of European imperialism and colonization, attacking
incidentally patterns of behavior which in part led to
the first great world conflict of our century. In a ritualistic journey of learning up the Congo, he has Marlow
discover that Kurtz, a symbol of European civilization
in his amazing intelligence, his artistic expressiveness, and
his humanitarian sense, is capable of avarice, lust, tyr-
anny, even murder. In fact, Conrad describes Kurtz's
decay and Marlow's journey to recognition of it in terms
that are at once as biological and as psychological as

those of any Darwin-and-Freud-influenced naturalist. "Going up that river," he writes, "was like traveling back to the earliest beginnings of the world, when vegetation rioted on the earth and the big trees were kings," as if he is designating an atavistic return to some stage of nature even before the animals and man evolved. Or again, on such a journey "one's past came back to one . . . in the shape of an unrestful and noisy dream." In a kind of nightmare he is recalling experiences suppressed and forgotten or facing the id, which has been hidden beneath the "monkey tricks" of honorific manners and occupations. Apparently Conrad could be fashionably scientific about the animal-part of man that even centuries of culture and years of education could not undo.

But the admission of a basic animalism in man and of the ineffectualness of learned controls did not destroy Conrad's faith in human nature. Within the limits of his story, he proves both logically for his own satisfaction and empirically for the satisfaction of his scientifically-minded contemporaries that man has a moral sense as *inborn* as the flesh and its passions. On the way up the Congo to the "heart of darkness," the natives working on the boat have carried with them a supply of "rotten hippo meat," which is soon exhausted by consumption and destruction. The accompanying pilgrims throw part of it overboard, theoretically because they cannot stand its odor but actually, says Marlow, because "you can't breathe dead hippo waking, sleeping, and eating, and at the same time keep your precarious grip on existence." The jungle is ironically having its effect on white men and professed Christians. Having lost their meat, the natives then exist on a minimum of food—so far as Marlow can see, on inadequate particles of half-cooked dough. He

wonders "why in the name of all the gnawing devils of
hunger they didn't go for us," for after all they were
taught cannibalism as strongly as the European was
taught humanitarianism. Marlow, in contemporary psychological terms, looks at them "with a curiosity of their
impulses, motives, capacities, weaknesses, when brought
to the test of an inexorable physical necessity." He discovers "something restraining," not "superstition, disgust, patience, fear—or some kind of primitive honor,"
but a kind of "scruple" beyond any "earthly reason."
His logical conclusion is that since the natives are dras-
tically hungry and since their learned mores do not
forbid eating other human beings, some *innate* restraint,
some natural moral sense, must exist in man even in his
most primitive state. If the symbolic savagery of Kurtz,
the educated European, illustrates the natural animality
of man despite his learned manners and morals, the restraint of the cannibals illustrates likewise the natural
scruple of man even if he has learned no morals, in the
traditional Western sense. The natives' control is de-
cidedly not the Freudian superego, that metaphor of
what the parents, teachers, preachers, and policemen
tell us is right, that learned shell of social direction. It is
more the universal reason glorified in the eighteenth and
early nineteenth century as a part of man, who served as
a battlefield for the hero reason and the villain passion.

One more point needs pursuing before Conrad
proves the *natural* dualism of man. If man can regress in
the manifold sense of Kurtz individually, or of Marlow
figuratively in his journey toward Kurtz, can man fallen
re-exercise his moral capacity? The structure of *Heart
of Darkness* takes the reader step by step from "civilization" to the center of the jungle where Marlow struggles

to save Kurtz, and thereby himself, as his constant admission of the "fascination of the abomination" suggests, and then step by step from the jungle back to the Western world, all within the vast and subtle structure of Marlow's time-full memory and timeless wisdom. On the way back Kurtz, dissipated, dying, a mere voice, literally and figuratively, looks into the depths of himself and whispers the terrible words of moral evaluation: "The horror, the horror." Conrad emphasizes again man's moral sense in the ability of the human being to observe his catastrophe and evaluate it with self-condemnatory confession. Certainly here is something akin to tragedy, not of the individual but of every man. ". . . then they very nearly buried me," says Marlow in complete identification with the European-trained Kurtz. Kurtz had "no restraint, no faith, and no fear," but struggled "with his soul" and reachieved in his self-evaluation "an affirmation, a moral victory paid for by innumerable defeats, by abominable terrors, by abominable satisfactions." It is this cycle of experience that demands from Marlow humble "loyalty to Kurtz" and in fact loyalty to himself, for it assures that whatever man does or whatever happens to him, as the case may be, he has the ability to cope with it in thoughts and words, to rise above it as it were. The experience of Kurtz is as cathartic for Marlow, and implicitly for the reader, as Aristotle declared that of the tragic hero to be for the members of the Greek audience.

Conrad has dramatically demonstrated a twofold nature of man compatible with the orthodox dualism of Christianity and countless other religious-and-philosophical traditions. There has always been the contention that the emphasis on Christ as both god and man and on man

as both the spirit and the body was in part the Greek
influence in an Hebraic culture. Plato's famous metaphor
pictured man as a celestial chariot driver of a team of two
horses, one horse, a milder, fairer one, naturally straining
upward and the other horse, a wilder, darker one, ever
tugging downward. The duty of the driver, a symbol
of man's innate reason and moral sense, was to keep the
two horses working together on a straight road through
the sky. Of course, it would be fine if both horses should
soar upward and land the driver on the top of Mount
Olympus with the gods. But the very nature of the wild
one made this an impossibility, and the admirable best
that the driver could aim at was to keep the disparate
horses working some compromise as a functioning team.
This twofold concept of man's nature hardly starts with
Plato or with any designated culture, for it is as old as
the prehistoric wonderings about how night becomes
day, how winter becomes spring, how man is born and
dies, only to leave a son behind him. Where does man
come from, where does he go, and how does he continue
the life on this earth? If winter becomes spring, man
dead must become man alive in some mysterious and
hence worshipful way. Even within the limits of Western culture, the familiar polar words for the dualistic
nature of man are manifold: soul and body, spirit and
flesh, immortality and mortality, the reason and the
passions, and so on to Conrad's "innate strength" and
"the jungle" within. Freud's id and superego are not the
same kind of opposition. Like the body, the flesh, the
passions, the id is tied up with the physical and hence
emotional make-up of man. But unlike them, it is in
itself a natural complex of both desirable and undesirable
elements according to conventional evaluations. The

superego, the metaphor for these evaluations, is a *learned* control in contradistinction to the *inborn* goodness or morality that soul, spirit, reason suggest. The orthodox religious concepts involve an acceptance on faith of an immortal spark that tempers the flesh and returns to the Immortal Spark after the flesh is dead. The thinking of the nineteenth century which Conrad was criticizing was monistic in its emphasis on scientific observation and prediction. The nearest the new naturalism came to religious reverence for a God reflected in the godhead was a somewhat timid agnosticism.

In my discussion of Steinbeck later, I emphasize the difficulty of maintaining the early naturalist position in practice. There is no such thing as objectivity in art or in anything else, but the young and self-conscious naturalists such as Zola in France and Frank Norris in America contended that there was. To them, the function of the artist was to describe, not to explain or to judge. At least this is what they said in their manifestoes, being forced by a kind of hydrostatic paradox of controversy into an extreme and stark stand. Literary manifestoes are always a kind of caricature in contrast to the actual practice of those who sign their names to blast at their more traditional contemporaries. Somehow the naturalist felt that if he were going to free himself from current myths about the universe, society, and man, he must first *describe* and be careful not to impose patterns. The patterns of life might be *induced* from described *facts;* they should not be accepted *on faith* and *in spite of.* Another illusion of the early naturalist was that he could develop and utilize a detached style compatible with his theme of detachment. Again, the proclamation that he would free himself of abstractions and subjective

pourings-out of self has led to an equation of so-called
realistic techniques with naturalistic theses. A self-pro-
claimed naturalist might start out *describing* his society,
but his very choice of words to convey the *awful* plight
of man reveals his feeling for man. A familiar pattern
was from "Here it is, like it or not" to "Here it is, you
can't like it, what shall we *do* to change it?" Or from
stating that God is Indifferent Hap instead of Benevo-
lent Reason to wondering, if man *is* in this fix, what each
man as a part of Man can do to relieve it even a little.
A recognition that man himself is not rational man in
control of his world involved experimentation in methods aimed at emphasizing the basically emotional nature
of man. Paradoxically, expressing most effectively the
emotions of natural man that the naturalist discovered
were the very impressionistic methods often contrasted
to the prosaic realism that the professed naturalists were
so proud of. Conrad, I should say, is bothered by the
theoretical naturalism and its self-conscious practice, the
new literary scientism in content and in technique. He
is bothered, in effect, by what the word *naturalist* continues to suggest to us at the first level of its meaning
even if we are aware of its inconsistencies in practice
and of its paradoxical development.

The only dualism conceivable for the strict naturalist was an external dualism between what man pretends
to do and what man does, as for example in the monopo-
list who preaches "free enterprise." And since to the
behaviorist, man is what he does, even this naïve dualism
vanishes. In 1929, *A Farewell to Arms* appeared significantly at the end of a decade of taken-for-granted
naturalism. In that very year, Joseph Wood Krutch
lamented forcefully that a non-dualistic concept of man

made tragedy in either the classical or the Renaissance sense an impossibility for creator or appreciator except as an academic problem. In tragedy, as has been suggested in the example of Kurtz, man is faced with catastrophe that some combination of God, the universe, society, and his own nature brings upon him. But the tragic protagonist proves that he is after all more than an animal: that he has free will, a moral sense, a place, albeit small, in a vast and supernatural order of things and that the creation which includes him is a dualistic creation. Without an implicit dualism, such as that which Conrad worked so meticulously to dramatize, the final catastrophe may be simply oppressive rather than ennobling and man may evolve as merely a pathetic creature, all the more foolish because his ideals are ridiculously high, misleading, or lacking.

Tragedy in one way or another is a religious mode and pathos is not. The very function of Greek tragedy in its original purpose as a part of the Dionysian festival, or its more sophisticated purpose as an artistic cathartic, is consciously spiritual. *Oedipus Rex*, for example, criticizes the belief in *physical* saviors. Young Oedipus, arriving cocksurely at Thebes, saves the city from the inscrutable monster, the Sphinx. To do so, he has answered: "man" to the Sphinx's bewildering question of what moves first on four feet, then two, then three, but is weakest when it moves on four. Oedipus then conducts himself as a melodramatic hero, accepting the thanks of the people and the traditional prize of a royal marriage and the throne. But the very point of the play is to remind us that physical saviors are as nothing beside the spiritual saviors who choose to become the scapegoats for all mankind and to do penance before the gods or God, as the case

may be, for man's manifold pride. It was impossible
for Oedipus as the youthful revitalizer of the impotent
city to accept the values of sacrifice, humility, faith
that he achieves by the end of the drama. These come
only with experience, and as Oedipus' answer to the
Sphinx should have told him, experience is an inevitably
crippling, hurtful, suffering experience, justifiable because it enables man to transcend the physical limitations
of his world and his flesh. To the early Greeks, the
story of Oedipus reflected that of Dionysus, whose joy-
ful resurrection after various associations with persecu-
tion and death was celebrated each spring in the theater.
Tragedy as the celebration of spiritual rebirth had to
assume man made in the image of God.

In our climate of cultural relativity it need hardly
be pointed out that Dionysus and Christ are alike the
suffering gods, the tragic gods, who go through the pain
and the exile of winter to become in spring the embodi-
ment of life that is stronger than death. It is as natural
for the Western writer of tragedy to make Christ his
objective correlative, against which he measures the
experience of man, as it was for the Greek playwright to
build his tragedy around the stories of Dionysus. Both
figures are topical dramatizations of the archetype of the
sacrificial hero.

For Conrad, who insisted on the innate nobility, the
symbolic godliness of man, in the face of a contrary
climate of opinion, the conception and the creation of
tragedy were practically a moral responsibility. This
obligation he fulfilled impressively in *Lord Jim*, the full-
length novel written at the turn of the century, a few
years after *Heart of Darkness*. Conrad implies his thesis
near the beginning of the novel when the seaman Jim is

being examined for his compulsive desertion of pilgrims
on a supposedly sinking ship. Again through Marlow,
Conrad insists that man's actions are somehow related to
his "soul" rather than to his "liver" and that there is
considerably more to man than the "facts" of his observable behavior. Marlow, incidentally, has already been
put through the journey of learning to the "heart of
darkness," which taught him so impressively the dualistic
nature of man. If we accept the statements of Jim's emotions on face value rather than as rationalizations, we
must agree with Conrad that his protagonist has some
sort of "soul," for Jim cannot live with himself until he
has done penance for his moral failure. In the person
of a minor character such as Brierly, the apparently perfect seaman who commits suicide when forced to judge
himself through Jim, Conrad emphasizes that the failure
of Jim is potentially the failure of every man and that
Jim in his own penance will become the scapegoat for
every man.

Conrad gives Jim the opportunity for a dedicated
life in an isolated world when he has the godlike Stein
assign him to the managership of Patusan, the settlement
up the river. Jim attempts to rule the people through
the techniques of love and understanding, but predictably his moral strength is his political weakness. Jim
refuses to liquidate the decadent faction of the Rajah
who formerly exploited the people, or to punish the
satanic Brown in whom he recognizes every man's pathetic situation, or to resist the leader of the people
whom he has served best, although he is wrongly blamed
for the death of the leader's son. Lord Jim, as the people
call him, is betrayed and finally killed as an evil spirit
by those to whom he has shown varying degrees of

kindness. He refuses the plea of his mistress-wife to
fight or to flee certain death, and slowly approaches the
old chief Doramin, the grieving father who wants venge-
ance for the death of his son Dain Waris. Marlow, as
usual, is narrating:

"He hath taken it upon his own head," a voice said aloud.
He heard this and turned to the crowd. "Yes. Upon my
head." A few people recoiled. Jim waited a while before
Doramin, and then said gently, "I am come in sorrow."
He waited again. "I am come ready and unarmed," he
repeated.

Marlow's epitaph for Jim expresses a conflict between
describing Jim on the one hand as a psychologically
convincing man and on the other as a veritable god who
has briefly visited the earth:

Now he is no more, there are days when the reality of
his existence comes to me with an immense, with an over-
whelming force; and yet upon my honour there are moments, too, when he passes from my eyes like a disembodied
spirit astray amongst the passions of this earth, ready to
surrender himself faithfully to the claim of his own world
of shades.
    Who knows? . . .

Earlier, Conrad has allowed Marlow a conjecture that
suggests the spiritual nature of tragic heroes even in
the Renaissance, when playwrights were more disposed
to a kind of secular dualism—if the phrase is not entirely
contradictory. ". . . is not mankind itself," asks Marlow,
"pushing on its blind way, driven by a dream of its
greatness and its power upon the dark paths of excessive
cruelty and excessive devotion. And what is the pursuit
of truth, after all?" The excesses which demand punish-

ment sound like a devious route to transcendence, but
Conrad and the traditional writers of tragedy point to
it as the only way. Holding on almost defiantly to his
dualistic concept of the nature of man, Conrad says in
effect: the story of Lord Jim has the elements of tragedy
if modern thinkers will allow as much. And in his very
imagery he implies that there is Christ in any tragic
figure regardless of the nature of his excess.

How has Conrad succeeded in conveying to his
reader meanings above and beyond but within the literal
level of his action? I should like to suggest one way.

The unique metaphor is related to wit: it is a play
on ideas through a play on words, the primary way after
all that we can demonstrate our conceptual play. The
phraseology of *play* immediately suggests the pun, which
in its single-word expression of differences tends to be
a kind of concentrated metaphor. The ordinary pun is
dull in that the likeness related to differences is simply
the obvious and coincidental one of the sameness of
sound, but the puns which are pivotal to dramatic art
involve meaningful likeness as well as ironic difference.
The significant artistic pun is related to metaphor, irony,
and—to throw us into another complex of ideas—symbolism. One might venture to suggest that effective drama
revolves around a central, dominating pun.

Before going on with *Lord Jim*, reconsider Conrad's
controlling pun in *Heart of Darkness*, that is, his use of
jungle and *civilization*. Conventionally, the Westerner
associates *civilization* with such externals as dress, furni-
ture, art, manners, mores, laws. The imagery with which
he traditionally surrounds his civilization is that of light
and whiteness which it is his mission to bring to darkness and blackness. In *Heart of Darkness* the ostensibly

civilized is the truly savage: Brussels, the European
center of the trading company, is a "whited sepulcher,"
a place of true darkness and true savagery. As the center
of the corrupt trading company, it is the heart of darkness in an important sense of the phrase. The civilized
man, climaxed in the overeducated Kurtz, is the chief
personification of savagery and darkness, the man who
gives in most completely to the jungle around and
within him. True civilization lies in the black cannibals,
who exercise intuitively their inner strength. One pun,
then, is *civilization;* another more complex pun is *jungle.*
Both words have extensional and intensional meanings
which deny each other.

Lord Jim employs the same pun in a way, but more
important imagery than that of *civilization* and *jungle*
has to do with *Western* and *Eastern* and, again, *white*
and *black.* Traditionally, to Conrad's English reader,
civilization, Western, and *white* are related in connotation as are *savagery, primitivism; Eastern, Oriental;
black, brown, colored. Lord Jim* is divided into two
parts. At the beginning Jim is one of a crew on a ship,
a separate world as Conrad describes it. As navigator, he
is entrusted with steering the pilgrims on their quest for
salvation through a visit to Mecca. The pilgrims are
colored, Oriental peoples; Jim is a white, Western man.
The other members of the crew are also white and
Western, forming with Jim a kind of microcosm of the
European macrocosm. An inscrutable crisis occurs at
sea, and Jim jumps, deserting his charge. Whether he
jumps compulsively or deliberately is beside the point.
The fact remains that, like the amoral ones who have
chosen to desert, Jim is guilty of jumping. Conrad surrounds the jumping from the ship into the boat with

fallen angel and *descent into hades* imagery. Jim has committed the damnable and is judged by a panel of men, who actually are no less condemnable than the next man, whatever their appearances may be. Jim, who starts life with romantic illusions of becoming a hero, specifically a *savior* of man in shipwrecks at sea, suddenly finds himself in the *same boat with other men,* indeed with the lowest of other men. More simply, one might say that he finds after all that he is a man, hence an inevitable traitor to his ideals and charges, damnable, guilty, low, fallen—if one likes—into the heart of darkness. Conrad suggests, with contempt for the phrase, that Jim the white man has failed to bear his burden of the colored pilgrims and, in serious tone, that Jim a man has failed to fulfill his responsibility to other men and to himself in this our world. The difference between Jim and the other crewmen in the first half of the book is that Jim faces formal judgment by a board of investigation whereas the others escape by amoral indifference, physical illness, and the convenient fantasies of delirium. Even so, the facing of judgment by law is not the essential distinguishing quality of Jim; it is his insistence on judging himself though the trial is over and done with and his identity is for all practical purposes hidden. Conrad starts with Jim's fall, or rather jump, and proceeds to reenforce Jim's insistence on self-flagellation unrelated to the public opinion of men. Then, halfway through the book, he has the godlike Stein isolate Jim from that part of the Eastern world with which Western "civilization" is constantly in touch. Once more Jim is in the position of figurative navigator in a microcosm of a world in which people depend on him as the bearer of their burdens. One almost thinks of the first half of the book as the Old Testament, in which man fails his responsibility and is driven from place to place as if seeking somewhere to hide his guilt. In this half of the book Jim is the archetypal Adam; he is clearly Everyman. Similarly, the second half of the book is a kind of New Testament, in which the protagonist is no longer Man but a god who assumes the shape of man to show him by a life of sacrifice the way to redemption. In this half of the book, as we have previously suggested, Jim develops as the archetypal Christ; he is clearly the sacrificial scapegoat for Everyman.

It is in the dualism of man's nature and the dualism of Christ-as-Man that Conrad employs his *white-and-black* pun. Consider *white* as the color of man's skin, as a synonym for Western as in "Western culture," as similar in connotation with *light* both as a shade and as a metaphor for truth, knowledge, goodness, as in association with *up, heaven, transcendence*. And consider *black* as the color of man's skin, as a synonym for *colored* as in the culture of the colored peoples, as similar in connotation with *dark* as a shade and a metaphor for ignorance, falsehood, depravity, as in association with *down, hell, damnation*. Now proceed to the series of ideas with which Conrad keeps playing. *White* men think themselves better than *black* men, but they are all *men*, neither better nor worse than each other, but all imperfect, *black* with the *white* speck of the soul, or whatever it is, tucked away somewhere in the *blackness* of the flesh and of the world. Under the illusion and pretense of thorough *whiteness* (for example, they rationalize their evil ways with such high-sounding statements as the *black* man is the *white* man's burden), they *must* express their *black* ways by virtue of their very nature,

which is both *black* and *white* but more easily the
former than the latter. Actually, the *white* speck is
brought out only by facing the truth of one's *blackness*,
accepting responsibility for it, suffering and sacrificing
for it. In this sense, Christ, the *white* one, appeared in
the guise of man, the *black* one; he alone was *truly* the
white man assuming the *black* man's, every man's,
burden and dying for it. Jim in the first half of the book
is a *white* man in the most naïve sense of the word, exist-
ing under the delusion that he is different from, better
than other men. In the last half of the book he becomes
the true *white* man in his giving of himself as the scapegoat for all men, *white* and *black*. Interestingly, the
final devil whom Jim faces is a *white* man named *Brown*,
who tempts and tests Lord Jim as Satan taunted Christ.
Marlow recalls his final sight of Jim in imagery pertinent to the dominant pun of color: "his smooth tan-and-
pink face with a white line on the forehead, and the
youthful eyes darkened by excitement to a profound,
unfathomable blue."

We can make Conrad's *black-and-white* pun inclusive if we extend its association to *Eastern* and *Occidental, death* and *life*. We need not take the time to do
so in any detail, but think of *Occidental* as a direction,
a section, a culture, as the place of the setting sun, as
literally falling, as death, as darkness, and think of *Oriental* as a direction, a section, a culture, as the place of
the rising sun, as literally rising, as birth and rebirth, as
the source of light. The ironies, the metaphors, the
clusters of imagery, the symbols, the supreme puns are
marvelously interwoven by Conrad.

In contrast to the hectic realism of the early naturalists, Conrad's methods were consciously subjective and

symbolic. Writers of fiction are inclined within the scope of their stories to talk about their methods either directly as omniscient authors or indirectly through the characters whom they create as central intelligences. In *Heart of Darkness*, for example, Conrad contrasts "the direct simplicity of the yarns of seamen" with the atypical story-telling of Marlow: "to him the meaning of an episode was not inside like a kernel but outside, enveloping the tale which brought it out only as a glow brings out a haze, in the likeness of one of these misty halos that sometimes are made visible by the spectral illumination of moonshine." This is a statement of an interest in mood, in overall effect, in the complex associations of a thing, the kind of less-academic impressionism for which Ryder the painter is known, rather than in the vividness and completeness of detail and the painfully chronological order of the self-consciously naturalistic school. The method is carried even further in *Lord Jim* where the superficiality of fact is the essential emphasis of the theme of dualism. "Facts! They demanded facts from him, as if facts could explain anything!" says Conrad about Jim's failure of his ideals in his apparently clear-cut desertion of the ship full of pilgrims. "The facts those men were so eager to know had been visible, tangible, open to the senses, occupying their place in space and time, requiring for their existence a fourteen-hundred-ton steamer and twenty-seven minutes to the watch," he writes later as if he is parodying the new realism of the literary scientists. But he adds, "they [the facts] made a whole that had features, shades of expression, a complicated aspect that could be remembered by the eye, and something else besides, something invisible, a directing spirit of perdition that dwelt within, like a malevolent soul in a detestable body." The attempt to define the "something else" makes for the weaving of events back and forth, a repetitiveness that grows out of the diligent search for understanding, a wealth of abstract and subjective words such as the naturalist tried to avoid. All in all, these add up to the implicit rejection of objectivity and the approach to a variety of stream-of-consciousness, despite the emphasis of critics on Conrad as a traditional writer. The traditionalism lies in the attitudes, in the orthodox dualism, the consequent concept of tragedy, the availability of Christ as a serious frame of reference, but the style that is most functional for these "non-factual" attitudes is almost a kind of literary impressionism.

The sense of something beyond the observable leads, too, to a conscious employment of symbolism. Answering a gentleman who had both criticized and praised his works, Conrad wrote in 1918:

Coming now to the subject of your inquiry, I wish at first to put before you a general proposition: that a work of art is very seldom limited to one exclusive meaning and not necessarily tending to a definite conclusion. And this for the reason that the nearer it approaches art, the more it acquires a symbolic character. This statement may surprise you, who may imagine that I am alluding to the Symbolist School of poets and prose writers. Theirs, however, is only a literary proceeding against which I have nothing to say. I am concerned here with something much larger. But no doubt you have meditated on this and kindred questions yourself.

So I will only call your attention to the fact that the symbolic conception of a work of art has this advantage, that it makes a triple appeal covering the whole field of life.

All the great creations of literature have been symbolic, and in that way have gained in complexity, in power, in depth and in beauty.

This brings us back to the imagery throughout *Lord Jim*, which persistently reminds us of Christ as a symbol of man's dualistic nature. ". . . a directing spirit of perdition that dwelt within, like a malevolent soul in a detestable body," may sound more Manichean than Christian. Still, there is certainly something mystical about God willing and Christ insisting upon the crucifixion, that climax of "perdition" that is followed, however, by absolution, also related to a "soul in a detestable body." The Christ-figure is, as we have suggested, a tragic-archetype, and despite the outline of mortal sin, absolution through sacrifice, and resultant immortality, the archetype assumes innumerable dramatic forms.

The form that the Christ-symbol takes is not irrelevant to the climate of opinion of a particular time or to the artist's unique experience, even though tradition or the collective unconscious or human nature or the laws of nature and society may delimit the different Christs with a significant likeness. Almost every important writer in our milieu has at one time or another utilized Christ as a *leit-motif* or as a major symbol. I am not referring to the flood of novels which attempt to recreate a facet of the Scriptures for better or for worse, such as *Ben Hur, Quo Vadis, The Nazarene, The Robe*, but to sincere books which enrich contemporary themes by the employment of the chief objective correlative of our culture. Symbolism may have become synonymous with literary experimentalism to a reading public which theoretically wants only a "good story" without "hidden meanings." Ironically, however, the most repeated cluster of symbols is abstracted from the traditional Christian lore, in which the popular reader of the Western World professes at least a vague belief. The correlative of Christ is the *something* through which the Western writer frequently gets at *everything*.

BIBLIOGRAPHICAL NOTE:

THE HISTORY OF IDEAS

Conrad's "Prince Roman" is included in the Viking *Portable Conrad* (New York, 1947) as is his letter to Barrett H. Clark which I have just quoted. The approaches to Conrad are manifold, but I am more interested in this chapter in approaches to tragedy such as Richard B. Sewall's *The Vision of Tragedy* (New Haven, 1959), Francis Fergusson's *The Idea of a Theater* (Princeton, 1949), and Bernard Knox's *Oedipus at Thebes* (New Haven, 1957). Joseph Wood Krutch's famous essay on "The Tragic Fallacy" was a chapter in *The Modern Temper* (New York, 1929), a book which talks about climate of opinion in an interesting and dramatically clear way that the writers of histories-of-ideas rarely achieve. In *The Modern Temper* Mr. Krutch is of course talking on a level and to an audience different from those of Arthur O. Lovejoy in his *Essays on the History of Ideas* (Baltimore, 1948), but in the end Krutch's kind of sincere and discursive book may be considerably more significant. George Santayana's "Tragic Philosophy," included in M. D. Zabel's edition of *Literary Opinion in America* (New York, 1937), is pertinent to our concern in this chapter both with tragedy and with the ideas implicit in literature. Charles Child Walcutt's *American Literary Naturalism: A Divided Stream* (Minneapolis, 1956) is a readable and valuable discussion of naturalism in idea and in practice.

III

Christ As Death-in-Life And Life-in-Death:

DOSTOYEVSKY'S
Crime and Punishment

IN ALL times and places the devil tends to take many shapes, but regardless of time and place the god invoked to exorcise the devil tends to take only one. This diversity of evil and uniformity of good may have to do with what Plato would call the imperfection and variety of matter and the ideality and universality of essence. The devil is topical and conventional: he is of this world, one which we know from experience or another which we know from newspapers, radio and television, history books, and research. Man's conception of him is what makes drama possible in more ways than one. *Dramatic* has primarily two connotations for us, the first pointing to content and the second pointing to method. The first implication, that of content, is that a cloistered virtue, a virtue untested, is undemonstrable, though it may be conceivable to the human mind. A positive and highly pertinent corollary, then, is that drama demands bringing virtue out of the cloister into the world, testing it obviously and recurrently—that is, drama implies tension, conflict, polarities of values, interdependent dichotomies. Indeed, I may be redundant on this point, for drama *is* by definition whichever of these phrases or similar ones appeal to the critical reader. The second implication, that having to do with method, follows from the first. Drama furthermore involves the reduction of the general to the specific. It is not ideas explicitly presented; it is ideas implicit in specific persons working out their face-to-face relationships against a specific background. Background in this sense is the theatrical backdrop with manifold dimensions: setting, yes; time and place, yes; but as much more than these as *climate of opinion* may suggest. The term *enveloping action*, which some critics prefer to *setting*, suggests the roundness of the surroundings in which credible characters act out related destinies. Man against these surroundings we may call *man in the conscious world*, say, Julius Caesar in the Rome of his time as Shakespeare, writing in the Renaissance, conceives it and as we, reading in the twentieth century, see the sixteenth-century creation of the first century B.C. Or Marlow and Kurtz in their literal contexts of late nineteenth-century Europe, Asia, and Africa as Conrad depicts the spheres of his contemporary experience. Or—to jump to those writers with whom we shall be presently concerned—Bazarov of *Fathers and Sons* (1862) and Raskolnikov of *Crime and Punishment* (1867) in the mid-nineteenth-century Russia of Turgenev and Dostoyevsky respectively.

To the serious writer, man in and of the world is fallible, whether the fallibility is to be laughed at (comedy and the comic modes), lamented (pathos), or recognized as a necessary step on the road to redemption (tragedy).

An important question is where to place the blame for man's imperfection. To make the problem melodramatically simple, we may believe in the basic goodness of man and attribute his corruption to society, that very *conscious world* in which man acts. Or we may believe in the animality of man and attribute his corruption to his own physiological-psychological-emotional nature. These theories of man may not be so opposed as they appear at first statement. Obvious questions are: if man is basically good, how can the society, a collective term for designating relationships between men, become corrupt; or if man is basically evil, should we blame a malignant god for creating him this way or the uncontrollable tricks of evolution for working themselves out in this way? The story of the Garden of Eden with its climax of original sin brings together the Romantic concept of the goodness-of-man-in-nature, the orthodox religious concept of the god-in-man, the Calvinist concept of the sin for which man must take responsibility and from which he must earn redemption, and the Darwinian concept of fiercely struggling man who must submit to agreed-upon external controls. A primary difference in theory is that of emphasis, but a primary likeness in literary application is that man in the conscious, observable, dramatizable world is evil. Whether he is redeemable or not is another question, though undoubtedly the finally important one.

Evil, then, is man-in-the-world. And man-in-the-world is what the author writes about on the level that first involves us emotionally. Through this involvement we may gradually learn that there are things beyond this our world, things unchanging and eternal. But whether we learn this or not, the world which we must enter before we have even the chance to learn it, makes possible the infinite variety of literature, which has, after all, only a few themes to treat. Indeed, if one defines theme traditionally as dominating conflict and pervading tone, that is, the author's attitude toward the parts of his conflict, serious literature may be said to treat only *one* theme, life and death, toward which authors assume a variety of attitudes.

For a moment, consider *Crime and Punishment* as a story of life and death. Raskolnikov is a young man of genteel background, though to be sure the cultural superstructure of his gentility is without the economic substructure from which it developed. Gentility in the characters who profess it, such as Raskolnikov's proper but impecunious mother and the poverty-stricken, sick, near-mad Katerina Marmeladov, is all airs and fantasy. It is understandable but nevertheless false pride. It is a form of decadence or, figuratively speaking, death. Raskolnikov is a young man in the process of education, for which his mother and sister, still with the air of gentility, will sacrifice the integrity of their emotions. As fanatically as his mother and Katerina believe in the superiority of their social positions in the remnant of feudal Russia, Raskolnikov consciously believes in the superiority of his intellect. This conscious belief is *his* devil, constantly at war with the unconscious, intuitive feeling for others and identification with them which he cannot repress, however much he may try. The separation of his conscious theorizing and his unconscious expression of self is so great that contemporary psychologists frequently point to him as a classic case of schizophrenia. The famous theory of his consciousness is a caricature of eighteenth- and early nineteenth-century rationalism. He contends that all men have the capacity of reason but that only a few men are courageous enough to utilize and apply it. Those few make history. They observe the plight of man, analyze it, determine and take necessary steps for remedying it. The new step which the superior ones take by way of changing the world, by way of "saving" mankind, is inevitably crime in the judgment of the *status quo*. But if it is successfully achieved, the step is a pioneering revolutionary act in the judgment of the new society which evolves. Raskolnikov's theory of the prerogative of the superior ones to use any means to contribute to the salvation of the inferior ones, even murder or massacre, subtly mocks such "peaceful" concepts as John Stuart Mill's belief that history is made by the decisions of rational men at the conference table and parodies such unrestrained concepts as that of Nietzsche's Super-Man. In its glorification of the reason, Raskolnikov's theory is literally rationalism, and in Raskolnikov's compulsion to prove it, it also involves empiricism. In its disdain of the emotions which the superior ones must absolutely repress if the new steps are to be taken, it has much in common with political Marxism, which sacrifices the means to the end, the present to the long view. It shares with laissez-faire capitalism the belief that man's selfish endeavor will somehow result in benefit to the public. It is pertinent to the new scientism, including the new psychology, in its emphasis on description not evaluation, the understanding of motivation not the judgment of the act. It foreshadows what of late has been designated atheistic existentialism with its translation of crime without punishment into freedom without social responsibility. In its extreme individualism free of involvement, it goes with Romanticism to the logical absurdity of physical hedonism. Dostoyevsky, then, has invented for Raskolnikov a way of thinking that suggests simultaneously almost every position of the modern intellectual, however dichotomous certain of these may seem in relation to each other. These opposing positions have in common the absence of God; they are the devil in his particular nineteenth-century guise. They are materialistic; hence they are non-spiritual. They are implicitly analytical, empirical, descriptive, existential; they have no place for faith. They are variously deterministic and individualistic, for they do not include bearing one's own cross and that of others as a way to redemption. Raskolnikov's theorizing makes strange bedfellows of fascism, communism, capitalism; rationalism and empiricism; determinism, existentialism, hedonism. Dostoyevsky's recognition of the likenesses in these overlapping and conflicting schools of thought is truly poetic in conception and execution. It is the discovery of similitude in dissimilitude which Wordsworth considered essential to the unique expression of man through poetry, a paradox which we have already associated with Conrad's use of the significant pun.

The absence of faith, sacrifice, redemption from the theorizing of Raskolnikov and from the theorizing of the lesser characters with whom he thinks he disagrees, is the paradoxical similitude to which I refer. The resultant irony gives the relationships which Dostoyevsky develops a figurative and provocative quality. Effective metaphor, in the last analysis, is a matter of ironic contrast, not literal comparison. The rational capacity of which Raskolnikov is so proud misses the sensitive point that he is guilty of the same mistakes of which his intellectual contemporaries are guilty.

Dostoyevsky's controlling metaphor and pun may

be even grander than Conrad's, for it deals unashamedly in the ironies of *life* and *death*. Raskolnikov's illusion is that the murder of the old pawnbroker will free himself and perhaps the world from oppression, will bring him *life* in the place of a *life of death*. But to Dostoyevsky any quest for *life*, for *salvation*, which omits God, faith, sacrifice is a mock-quest for further *death* under the illusion of *life*. Sonia, who ultimately redirects Raskolnikov to the true quest, reiterates at a climactic point of the novel the story of Lazarus, which is perhaps the most succinct dramatization of the *death and life* pun in the Judeo-Christian Scriptures. Literally a man *dead* returns to *life* through faith in Christ. But the parable equates our *life* with Lazarus' *death* and our *death* with his return to *life*. In *mortality* we shall gain *immorality* if we have faith in Christ and his teachings.

The convolutions of the life-death pun, the most comprehensive pun of all, are endless, and Dostoyevsky has utilized a remarkable number of them, both consciously and unconsciously. Man is born to die. He dies a thousand times. Each step of learning moves to the death of one part of the self and the birth of another, which in turn will die. The final step is physical death, the fitting climax of the death we have lived and the only way to true birth. We are born then into death and spend our lives, or deaths, seeking life, which we may find only at death. The inevitability of death and the potentiality of life are constantly at war within man— and on every possible level that the words can be read.

The specific religious imagery of Dostoyevsky has been much discussed. It is meticulous and melodramatic, and paradoxically it is enmeshing and effective. From the early definition of Raskolnikov's room as a tomb and of the city as "as stifling as his room" to Raskolnikov's final illness during Lent and recovery after Easter, we are playing with the ironies of death and life in the most orthodox sense.

One more point: Lord Jim was a seaman, and to make him a *man*, Conrad had to allow him the worst crime a seaman could commit. What else but *desert his ship?* Dostoyevsky's terms are broader: he immediately lets Raskolnikov commit murder by way of exemplifying the sins to which pride will lead. And what of Sonia, the savior to Raskolnikov's Lazarus? It has been pointed out that Sonia is a diminutive for Sophia, and that Sophia in the Greek-Orthodox religion is added to the Trinity as a kind of female principle suggesting both Wisdom and Love, almost in the sense of the Love that surpasseth Understanding. To make Sophia into an active agent in the novel, that is, to give the spirit flesh, Dostoyevsky lowers her in a dramatic equation to Christ's assuming the flesh. Lower the son of God and he becomes a man; lower the seaman and he deserts his ship; lower reasoning man and he commits murder. Lower the woman and she becomes the prostitute. We return repeatedly to the realization that art is an abstraction from experience, a pointing up of experience, in a sense a caricature of experience. It is always skirting melodrama, though one of the standards of artistry is the avoidance of melodrama while flirting with it. Dostoyevsky is hardly unaware of the melodramatic quality of his drama. "Think of it," he says directly to his reader when presenting fallen man faced with his redeemer, "think of it: in the same room a murderer and a prostitute!" It is as if he himself is astounded at the nakedness of the specifics into which he has reduced his generalizations.

The Greek-Orthodox Sophia, the female principle of Love and Wisdom, is like a foreshadowing of the assumption of the Virgin into the company of the Father, the Son, and the Holy Ghost. She functions in *Crime and Punishment*, as we have said, as a kind of female Christ to Raskolnikov's Lazarus. But to be sure there are differences between gods and goddesses as there are differences between men and women, and these differences are related to the natural, that is, physical and emotional, distinctions of the sexes and the consequent archetypes they assume. The role of woman has ever been threefold: (1) virgin or maiden, (2) the raped one or mate and wife, (3) the mother loving and suffering when those whom she has borne in pain and reared with care are hurt or inevitably separated from her. Mary of the Immaculate Conception is a wonderful combination of the three: the Virgin, the Madonna, the lamenting Mother at the tomb. Christ reminds us that man is born to die, and Mary that woman is born to suffer, perhaps the harder fate of the two, born to suffer the initial union with man, the labor of child-birth, the ups-and-downs, the deaths of husbands and sons. In a true sense Sonia displays the threefoldness of the archetypal woman: she is the pure, the virginal prostitute, and she is the little mother, in a grandly old syle Russian manner. Poor father, she says of the drunken and dying Marmeladov, who has failed to support her. Poor mother, she says of the mad and dying Katerina, who has with a word driven her to prostitution. Poor children, she says of her step-brothers and sisters when she pictures for them the fates of poverty and prostitution that she has endured. And poor, poor man, she says of Raskolnikov when he confesses to murder, and when, indeed, she has every right to be lamenting her own plight instead. Poor, poor man, she says, and offers him two crosses, one of death and one of resurrection, which he must bear for himself.

In doing so, Sonia, a kind of female savior in the guise of fallen woman, points the way of salvation to Raskolnikov, fallen man. Dostoyevsky makes the orthodox point that to be absolved by the suffering of the scapegoat, we must imitate the scapegoat in his sacrifices, his humility, his love. We must be willing to accept punishment for the crime of being a man, whatever form our manners may take.

I have tried to make three points with respect to *Crime and Punishment*. First: The evil with which the protagonist copes, either within or without him, is the specific dramatization of particular men in particular societies, that is, the drama of man in the conscious world. The devil with which we are warring in the great literature is of our world or at least of the worlds which we intellectually know and sophisticatedly relate to ours. Second: The interesting irony of great literature revolves around a kind of paradoxical pun: the conscious, waking world in which we endeavor for recognition of our material success, our intellectual superiority, and our exemplary lives, we think of as the best of all possible worlds, as *life*, as the light of truth, but it is a trap of the soul, the true *death*, the darkness in which we should be questing light. The enveloping action of Western literature allows frequently other related puns: the white world of ostensible progress is the black world of the heart for which we must bear responsibility if we are to be redeemed. Or again, the West of technical superiority is, alas, the West as the symbol of death without resurrection; in the West, we should be seeking the spiritual

East, the source of life, the eternal light and warmth, the recurrent rising. Third, and last: The way to the repressed unconscious, to the lost Eden, to the true light, to the symbolic East, the way to redemption, that is, from the sin of being men in the conscious world, is pointed out by the ideal of the sacrificial savior. That we can imitate him at all requires that we see him almost literally. To look at the god directly is to be blinded. The god must assume, for the purpose of reaching us and demonstrating to us the exemplary life, the guise of man. The Soul must dress the soul in the flesh. The Transcendent One must descend to the earth. The great Unconscious must shine through the conscious world. The Light must clothe itself in darkness. The Resurrection must be the Death *and* the Resurrection, and the End *and* the Beginning. A sense of the realities of the society, the capability of unique wit, the ability to dramatize an ideal—these make great literary art.

BIBLIOGRAPHICAL NOTE:

THE SYMBOLS OF RELIGIOUS RITUAL

An excellent example of the examination of symbolism in Dostoyevsky is G. Gibian's "Traditional Symbolism in *Crime and Punishment*," *PMLA*, December, 1955. Studies in religious symbolism such as Rollo May's *Symbolism in Religion and Literature* (New York, 1960), based on the summer, 1958, issue of *Daedalus*, lead one to an awareness of literature itself as ritual incorporating the recurrent images of religious ceremony as we recall it and know it. A study of the mass as drama can tell one a tremendous lot about the structure *and* the themes of every literary genre. In an essay in the winter, 1958-1959, issue of Washington and Jefferson College's literary magazine *The Wall*, William James discusses as mass Eliot's play *Murder in the Cathedral*, which by the very nature of its content and form invites the comparison, but novels seemingly as sprawling as the great nineteenth-century ones are often as structured as ritual if the reader responds to the symbolic guides whether employed consciously or unconsciously. A helpful guide to the symbolic guides is Ernest Lehner's *Symbols, Signs, and Signets* (Cleveland, 1950).

IV

Christt As The Archetypal Son:

TURGENEV'S
Fathers and Sons

CHRISTIAN symbolism bristles on the surface of *Crime and Punishment* as literally a part of the conscious world, in which on the other hand varieties of the new intellectualism are denying religion. The talk about Christ, God, the New Jerusalem, Lazarus, and crosses is explicit, and even when the religious frame of reference is implicit, it exists just below the surface of literal action. One might accuse Dostoyevsky of the imposition of a religiously symbolic framework upon his story if it were not a natural part of the climate of opinion which he depicts. It is furthermore an integral part of his theme. It is prepared for, recalled, and reaffirmed constantly by highly effective descriptions of behavior. Again, one hesitates to say *credible* patterns of behavior, for constantly the drama tends to become melodrama. The starkness of the conflict is not impertinent to the conspicuousness of the symbolism.

The Christian symbolism of *Lord Jim*, on the other hand, gradually dawns on one as Conrad weaves his intricate patterns of imagery into a tight tapestry of nar-

rative and meaning. A thread flashes here and is picked
up there, suggesting a related thread which has crossed
it subtly at some point already responded to. To see a
whole evolving is often difficult, but soon one is ex-
citedly recalling delicate details noticed and yet missed
and seizing upon a repetition of similar details suddenly
apparent through the imaginative variations which the
weaver has created.

There are really two symbolic methods demonstrated by Dostoyevsky and Conrad. The former tends
to use the conspicuous guide to meaning at a pivotal dramatic point. Sonia reads the story of Lazarus to Raskolnikov, and Lazarus becomes clearly the objective correlative for much that has already happened and much that
will happen. The very story of Lazarus becomes a dominant analogy and a pervading symbol. Conrad's symbolism grows out of an accumulation of similar images.
A cluster of *Lucifer* images, of *hell* images, of *descent* or
falling or *jumping into the abyss* images gradually en-
meshes the reader in a sense of reading about plain Jim,
then Lord Jim at war with the devil, within and without, and directs us, with many other clusters, to realize
that we have been reading the universal morality play
coincidentally set at sea. It is as if Dostoyevsky, conditioned to the religious ritual and lore of his environment,
used these deliberately and strikingly to give his story
structure, a symbolic frame, an explicitly stated theme.
On the other hand, it is as if Conrad, as strongly immersed
in these frameworks, wrote his story as a seaman first of
all and let his ready pattern of symbolism impinge on it
when it would. I once heard a distinguished woman
short-story writer say that she had never used a piece of
"conscious symbolism" in her life and then, when chal-

lenged that the story under discussion would have no
form and no meaning without an understanding of
Christian ritual, answer, "Well, I suppose I have never
used an important detail that was not an *unconscious*
symbol in some way." The distinction between the conscious and the unconscious is specious. It is as if Dostoyevsky's skill, or conscious use of religious symbolism,
dominates his unconscious creation, and as if Conrad's
sincerity, or unconscious use of religious symbolism,
subtly hides his skillful control of structure and detail.
Joyce finds a meaningful and ironic relationship between
the words *artificer* and *artist*. While Dostoyevsky is having tremendous impact on us, we nevertheless say frequently: "No, not that old chestnut!" And while Conrad
is slowly drawing us to the "kernel" in the middle of the
"haze," we wish occasionally for a chestnut to let us
relax from the subtle and wonderful and exhausting demands he places upon us.

Turgenev's *Fathers and Sons*, from which evolves a
pattern of similar religious implications, is strikingly different in effect and perhaps in method from both *Crime
and Punishment* and *Lord Jim*. In Turgenev, the conscious world, the evil which must be exorcised, is the
deliberately nihilistic position of his protagonist Bazarov,
a young Russian just out of medical training at the university. Bazarov is described by his fellow-student and
disciple Arkady as "a nihilist . . . a man who does not
bow down to any authority, who does not accept any
principle on faith, however much that principle may be
revered." Bazarov more than affirms this description of
himself, for in a consistently detached way he decries
faith, the reason, religion, art, the beauties of nature, abstract science, devotion to one woman, feminism, indi-

vidual responsibility, the belief in the common man, revolution, and even the application of medical knowledge to ailing persons. He says that he believes only in the frogs which he collects for dissection, observation under the microscope, and classification, and he claims that he is interested in individuals and in social systems only for the same purposes. The extreme rationalism of Raskolnikov is elusively recalled, but Raskolnikov's rationalization for his annihilation of a human being was at least the moral one of saving mankind. Bazarov says that all of the old must be destroyed before the new can be created, but he professes no commitment to the new. In fact, apropos the Russia in which Turgenov lived, he looks at the vulgar, ignorant peasants and dismisses them as not worth dying over or even practicing medicine on. As Raskolnikov cannot prevent the feeling of compassion for which his theory of crime without punishment has no place, Bazarov finds himself ultimately attracted to one Madame Anna Odintsov, but their mutual discipline of detachment and a complex of circumstances hinder the consummation of any feeling.

Although Turgenev is as critical of intellectual detachment as is Dostoyevsky, his central intelligence Bazarov is in a kind of frigid control of himself throughout most of the novel, in sharp contrast to the intensely emotional, mad Raskolnikov. The result is a highly economic, understated, direct dramatization of the devils which must be driven out. A part of the economy and restraint of Turgenev's method is the comparative absence of images and figures. The striking pivotal detail of Dostoyevsky and the intricate clusters of imagery of Conrad are not present to direct us to either an overlaid or an underlying pattern of religious symbolism, but interestingly enough a similar pattern emerges in *Fathers and Sons*. I shall review the narrative briefly to suggest how an awareness of the Christ motif develops for the reader.

Bazarov enters the novel as a trained doctor, but he is interested only in science for the sake of science, not in the application of modern medicine to the peasants who pay lip service to it but persist in dependence on their superstitions for cure. By admission Bazarov is uninterested in becoming a healer of mankind, nor is he interested in any social theories aiming at the salvation of humanity. He is immediately in conflict with the father and uncle of Arkady, a young romantic as the name suggests, who imitates Bazarov verbally if unconvincingly. Nikolai, Arkady's father, is extremely aware of his son's "new" education and would like to be a liberal, free, young thinker himself. His brother Pavel, by contrast, is a decadent leisure-class son of the old feudal aristocracy and at war with any questioning of the already disintegrating feudal tradition. While Arkady has been away at college, his father Nikolai has had an affair with Fenichka, his housekeeper's daughter, who bears him a son. He has set her up in his household devotedly and affectionately, but apologetically and fearfully before his aristocratic brother Pavel and his educated son Arkady. Arkady, as a conscious "new" thinker, accepts the relationship between his father and his mistress. Pavel, the self-conscious aristocrat, disdains Fenichka as not good enough for his family, but is drawn to her as a reminder of his former mistress, a Russian princess. Bazarov, visiting at Arkady's home, is fascinated with Fenichka—he would say as with a frog under a microscope. Here is one complex of characters:

Arkady, the new, educated, naïvely liberal thinker;
Nikolai, his father, trying hard to keep up with his son
by working at liberalism; Pavel, Arkady's uncle, flip-
pantly adhering to the old feudal manners despite the
disintegration of the economic substructure on which
they are based; and Bazarov, the thorough nihilist, at war
with Nikolai and with Pavel.

A second complex of characters includes Madame
Anna Odinstov and her young unmarried sister Katya.
Although at first Arkady is fascinated with Anna as a
sophisticated, "new" woman and Bazarov with Katya as
a virginal young woman worth experimenting with, ultimately Bazarov and Anna sense an attraction toward
each other and Arkady and Katya become engaged.
Anna has made a previous profitable marriage without
love and has had the good fortune to be left rich by her
deceased husband. She has in effect prostituted herself
legally and respectably. Experienced and hardened, she
faces the approaches of Bazarov, the deliberate nihilist.
They miss love because they know too much, because
they are old in more ways than one, and finally because
it is too late: Bazarov dies just when they may be on the
verge of admitting their attachment to each other.

A third complex of characters is Bazarov, his
mother Arina, and his father Vassily. After journeying
from the university to the home of Arkady and from
the home of Arkady to that of Madame Odinstov,
Bazarov arrives at the country homestead in which his
elderly mother and father reside. His father Vassily,
trained as a doctor like his son, runs his small estate with
gentleness and kindness to the peasants and with homely
but careful attention to their physical ailments. The
mother Arina is an affectionate and humble woman, full
of peasant superstitions and of the maturity which comes

with experience and suffering. Vassily and Arina endure unwillingly but resignedly the separation from their only son Bazarov.

Bazarov is a kind of catalyst for the three groups of characters. He is challenged to a duel by Pavel, who accuses him of flirtation with Nikolai's mistress Fenichka. Pavel is wounded slightly, but the absurdity of the situation, which Bazarov points out to him, leads Pavel to urge the marriage of Nikolai and Fenichka and to withdraw to live out his dilletantish life abroad even though he is aware of its futility. Bazarov is moved to make physical advances to Anna; she responds as if insulted, but the incident gives her insight into the pathos of her aloneness and leads her to give up Arkady to Katya. She makes a second fashionable marriage and accepts the emptiness which is her destiny. Attending the ill serfs of his father, Bazarov ironically contracts a disease and dies. His last words recognize the frustrations of his own existence and the enduring worth of his parents' lives.

In the details of plot which I have reviewed are three apparent motifs, all significantly relevant to the pattern of Christ. I should point out again that in *Crime and Punishment* and in *Lord Jim* the Christian imagery is definitely present, in each in its own way. In *Fathers and Sons* it is not so much specific imagery as analagous overall patterns that in one sense are *in* the material under discussion but in another sense simply *parallel* to it. Some critics would contend that it is "legitimate" to pursue what is integral but "illegal" to pursue what is parallel. I wonder that a clear-cut distinction can be made if the reader intuitively and intellectually makes the associations as he reads.

The first motif is that of *Bazarov as the doctor*. We

have mentioned that in his nihilistic stage, he is interested only in the dissection of people as of frogs, not in healing man or contributing to the salvation of mankind in any physical or social sense. At this point the spiritual is not even a question. Bazarov is completely disdainful of sacrifice of any kind on the part of one man for another. This is Bazarov, the young intellectual, man in the conscious world, man possessed with the contemporary devil if the author's understated tone is accepted. Bazarov's father, we are told, is hardly a brilliant doctor, but he devotes his learning and his feeling for the pain of others to helping the oppressed peasants around him. His life is literally one of constant service. Bazarov's grandfather, dead before the book begins, was a village priest, to whom the peasant came for help in the ills of the body as well as of the soul. As he is described, the phrase *medicine man* would aptly connote his twofold function. Take these overlapping terms for our pivotal pun: *medicine man, doctor, healer.* In the background of Turgenev's story is an entire history of the Russian culture or, more to the point, of any culture: from the dependence on faith for the cure of all ills, physical, emotional, spiritual, to a separation of the functions of priest and doctor, to indeed rejection of the priest on the part of the intelligentsia and dependence on the doctor alone. Father Alexei, a Greek-Orthodox priest who enters the novel briefly, is a kind of emasculated priest in his apologetic fawning before Bazarov's learning. Bazarov's development into a true doctor is highly ironic. Unlike Raskolnikov and Lord Jim, Bazarov is on no kind of conscious quest, neither a misdirected one nor a respectful one. He even resists practicing the medicine he has learned. In this attitude almost like Raskolnikov, he considers man not worth treating as an individual in a face-to-face relationship. Ultimately, he finds himself in the agony of aloneness, a plight which in his deliberate nihilism he has chosen for himself. He returns to the farm of his elderly mother and father and is soon helping his father treat the peasants. This is in spite of his conscious attitudes; he would even say that he does so not out of humanity, but out of curiosity. In an autopsy on a dead serf, Bazarov cuts himself, contracts the infection, and dies from blood poisoning. Add to our pun of *medicine man, doctor, healer*, the "logical" next step of scapegoat and/or savior. In spite of himself as man in the conscious world, in spite of the devil within and without him, Bazarov becomes a *true* doctor in much the same sense that his father has been all along. The Christ analogy need hardly be pointed out.

I have said that Turgenev's religious imagery is sparse beside that of Dostoyevsky or Conrad, but it is not altogether lacking. During Bazarov's death scene, the peasants sacrifice a loudly crowing cock. In his near delirium Bazarov dreams that he is a black cock chased by red dogs. The vicarious bloodletting of the peasant ritual may not literally cure Bazarov of his corruption, but it comes simultaneously with his unchosen and meaningful sacrifice. His final words to his parents urge that they take advantage of their "strong religious faith," and his final words to Madame Odinstov are words of love, humility, and belief in the exemplary lives of his parents. Father Alexei performs the final sacrament over him. Bazarov gives a shudder of horror, and Vassily shouts hoarsely: "I said I should rebel! . . . And I rebel, I rebel!" Are, then, the conscious, intellectual self and the un-

conscious, loving self in conflict until the very end? Does
Bazarov, despite his sacrifice, die in abject nihilism, noth-
ingness, death as a finality? His parents mourn, and
Turgenev ends the novel with assuring imagery:

Can it be that their prayers and their tears are fruitless? Can it be that love, sacred devoted love, is not all
powerful? Oh, no! However passionate, sinful or rebellious
the heart hidden in the tomb, the flowers growing over it
peep at us serenely with their innocent eyes; they tell us
not only of eternal peace, of that great peace of "indifferent" nature; they tell us also of eternal reconciliation and of
life without end.

In spite then of being a man, in this particular
dramatization a man guilty of the skeptical, materialistic,
deterministic thinking of the mid-nineteenth century,
Bazarov suffers for others. In his suffering he preaches
love, humility, faith, understanding. He dies the death
of the scapegoat. Turgenev surrounds his death with
the imagery of immortality. Raskolnikov, consciously
trying to prove himself a savior of mankind through the
exercise of his reason, approaches redemption when he
faces punishment for being a man, rational and/or irra-
tional. Lord Jim, seeking to be a savior of mankind
through the romantic dreams of heroism, attains true
heroism when he gives himself to be sacrificed for the
sins committed by all men, himself and others. Bazarov,
intensely denying his commitment to any quest for
values, nevertheless transcends the nothingness of his
existence by sacrifices which he makes without admittedly choosing to make them. Dostoyevsky and Conrad are conscious of the original mock-quests of their
protagonists and use religious imagery deliberately to
emphasize the inverted search and the ultimate true

search. The pattern of mock-quest into true quest, or
man into man-redeemed or near-god, is as strong in
Turgenev. But the resistance of Bazarov to seek anything, that is, his discipline of detachment which per-
vades the very style of the book, restrains his creator's
use of traditional symbols to point up his meaning. Even
so, the Christ pattern is clearly present and pertinent to
Turgenev's theme.

The pun of *priest-medicineman-doctor-healer-
scapegoat-savior* leads us to a second motif. I am reminded of Eliot's *Cocktail Party*. You will recall that in
Eliot's play the central figure is a psychoanalyst, who
combines effectively the function of priest and doctor.
Of the three figures whom the analyst treats within the
scope of the play, one achieves a meaningful death
through service and sacrifice to others, but the other two
are condemned to live out their lives with the destinies
they have chosen. Before their experience with the psychoanalyst, all three had pursued romantic cures for their
emotional ills, but after he worked with them, all three
saw themselves for what they were and accepted the necessity of each one's taking responsibility for the existence which preceded him. Only one had the capacity to
transcend this existence—and this is hardly made convincing by Eliot's choice of "crucifixion near an ant-
hill" as the incident to illustrate transcendence. The
very improbability of a final supreme sacrifice, which
Eliot describes rather than dramatizes, may suggest that
only the elect are saved and that few earn election.
Recognition and endurance of the Waste Land to which
we are condemned by the very fact of our being men
may be the most for which we can hope. Bazarov, practically the archetypal devil at the beginning of *Fathers*

and Sons, is extreme enough in his *fall* to become the archetypal Christ in the end. Pavel and Madame Odinstov, whom Bazarov unwittingly leads to self-discovery, continue their lives respectively as dilletantish expatriate and fashionable wife—a hell all the harder to bear because they have been directed to see it as hell. I mention this pattern because it is highly relevant to the relationship between the reader and the Christ-figure in any novel. In Eliot, is identification possible with Lavinia and Edward, the cocktail-party-giving couple, or with Celia, Edward's mistress turned missionary? In Turgenev, do we more readily see ourselves in Pavel and Anna, the sophisticated, educated, well-mannered, decadent ones, or in Bazarov, the Lucifer *and* the Christ? Who after all is fortunate enough to approach the godhead?

The pathetic decadence of Pavel and Anna brings us by way of contrasts to a third motif, one which the title emphasizes. The most familiar translation of the title is *Fathers and Sons;* a more exact one perhaps is *Fathers and Children.* Let us vary the first term for a moment, and call it *Parents and Children.* Bazarov's parents are truly the archetypes of the inevitable father and mother, a destiny which they accept as all mature men and women must. Arina, the mother, does not question the social order; she has read little and long since forgotten the bit of music and French she was taught. She is devoted to her husband and loves and fears her son, fears him because he is educated and full of new ideas. Her own attitudes are a combination of folk superstitions, which find a basis of truth in the nature of man and in nature, and of common sense and intuition, which find a basis of truth in the heart. Still, it is from the unsophisticated Arina that one of the great truths of the book comes:

A son is broken off. He's like a falcon that flies home and flies away again when it wants; but you and I [she addresses her husband] are like mushrooms growing in the hollow of a tree, we sit side by side without moving from the same place. Only I will never change for you, and you will always be the same for me.

She is the final step which all true women must reach. Recall our description of Sonia in *Crime and Punishment* as virgin, the raped one, mother on the one hand and as eternal Wisdom and Love on the other. In *Fathers and Sons* the threefold function of woman is segmented into Katya, the romantic heroine; Fenichka, the seduced one who becomes mother and wife; and Arina, the mother who must endure the tearing of the child from the womb in figurative ways too many to recount. On the occasion of the final tearing away of Bazarov in literal death, Arina reminds one not of Mary the Madonna, but of the role for which the calmly smiling Madonna is destined: Mary waiting and mourning outside of the tomb. Or Mary in the traditional *Pieta*, with agony and love on her face and her son not a babe in arms but a sacrificed man stretched across her lap. Woman is born to suffer: the pertinent pun is *labor-suffer-endure*.

It is this true destiny of woman which Madame Odinstov is attracted to, but which she resists. She is naturally affectionate and full of a gentle strength, but she is consciously intellectual and materialistic. She matches her wits with men, and she approaches marriage as a business. She wants love, but she is afraid of it as hurtful and impractical. In her two marriages to elderly, wealthy men she avoids the painful rape of the body through which woman earns her creativity. Her deliberately profitable marriages are instead the rape of the soul. Ironically, the result is more painful when she is forced to discover her plight and to live knowingly with it: empty and alone. Having a husband to comfort and a son to mourn are hardly happy fates; but they imply belonging in life and immortality thereafter.

If woman is born to suffer, man is born to die. These are the roles men and women play in the great dramas of all levels: experience, ritual, mythology, and literature. Once again, the *Pieta* composed of Mary the Mother and Christ the Son makes clear the working out of their true roles by Arina and Bazarov. But what of Vassily, Bazarov's father? The first members of an older generation with whom Bazarov comes into contact are Nikolai and Pavel, Arkady's father and uncle respectively. One has an immediate sense of the war between generations and of the pathos of the older generation trying to adjust to and cope with the newer. We have previously mentioned Oedipus. In the archetypal story of the hero, fathers are frequently told by oracles that the sons whom they have produced will replace them. This is a highly understandable dramatization of the natural cycle of things, but in each case the father tries to resist the inevitability of change. He sends his son off to die (notice that he is always unable to perform the murder himself), but as sons do, the son survives, kills the father without choosing to do so, and succeeds him. The fact that the son, now at the head of the household, becomes a father, only to face the same problems of change and death, need not concern us at the moment. The archetypal father, essential to the reproduction of the son, becomes frequently a symbol of authority without love. The son survives in spite of him and because of the protectiveness of his own mother, or Mother Nature, or some natural creature such as a shepherd much less involved in the affairs of the conscious world than the actual father. The war between father and son is not delimited by any particular environmental context. It is apparently true for all places and all times on the social level and on the personal, physiological, psychological one. Pavel, though in his cultural sterility he is not an actual father, is nevertheless a father figure in that he represents the manners and attitudes of a dying cultural framework. Bazarov, as the destroyer of authority, fights him head-on attitudinally and literally in a duel which grows out of their tacit contest over Fenichka. Through the duel, Pavel becomes resigned to the inevitability of social change and of his own "death." In several senses Pavel denies the mature role of man as the father at first, but moves, however slightly, in its direction. Nikolai, Arkady's father, tries hard to keep up with the times. He bones up on "new" ideas in anticipation of his son's return from the university, and he tries liberal measures on his plantation, resulting—according to Turgenev's tone—in a kind of emasculation of the system from which he comes. To be sure, he is disturbed by the "new," but he is apologetic for his attachment to the "old." He tries to be a true father, and Arkady, in spite of his conscious attitudes, feels affection for Nikolai. They do not even argue over the rights of Nikolai's infant son by his mistress Fenichka, though Bazarov warns that brothers like fathers and sons are at constant war with each other. Along this line, it might be pointed out that Bazarov in his farewell to Arkady addresses him as "brother" in spite of his having continually pooh-poohed the implications of the word socially and personally.

But back to Bazarov's actual father Vassily. Vassily's father, remember, was a village priest, and Vassily became an army doctor. One can imagine that Vassily and his own father were once in attitudinal conflict similar to that between Vassily and Bazarov, though Vassily's personality as it has evolved hardly lets us conceive this earlier stage in his development. In any case, within the scope of the book, Vassily is the *true* father as much as Arina is the *true* mother, and both of these roles are hard ones to bear. Arina has to comfort Vassily when he cries out in his despair at the hostilities of Bazarov or at literal separation from him or finally at the separation of death. But Vassily understands the inevitability of these difficult facts, and Turgenev allows him a succinct statement of them. Vassily is addressing Bazarov and Arkady:

> In this province . . . of course, gentlemen, you know better; how could we keep pace with you? You are here to take our places. Even in my time, there was a so-called *humoralist* Hoffmann and a certain Brown with his *vitalism* —they seemed very ridiculous to us, but they, too, had great reputations at one time. Someone new has taken Rademacher's place with you; you bow down to him, but in another twenty years it will probably be his turn to be laughed at.

Bazarov answers with the cocksureness of a young Oedipus, forgetting that even the microscope would reveal that man on two feet is followed by man on three:

> For your consolation I can tell you that we nowadays laugh at medicine altogether and bow down to nobody.

In another fifty pages Bazarov has fallen without choosing to and implicitly ascended without consciously knowing so.

The three motifs have coalesced: the scapegoat motif, the Waste Land motif, the old champion-new champion motif, unified by the involvement of Bazarov in the dramatization of each.

The Christmas, 1956, issue of *Life* magazine, devoted to "the American woman," emphasized the important part that the denial of archetypal roles plays in the disintegration of the family. "Men are designed by nature to sire children and women to bear them," stated an article on "Changing Roles in the Modern Marriage," "and from these elementary facts, psychiatrists say, come their differences in emotional needs. For women, the sexual act itself implies receptiveness and a certain passivity, while the long period of human gestation and the extraordinarily long period of a child's dependence implies a need for protection and support for the mother. These passing feminine qualities—receptivity, passivity, and the desire to nurture—color a woman's entire emotional life. . . . Since the male's primary function is simply to impregnate he can feel somewhat detached from the result, yet one of the significant ways in which male humans differ from, say, male monkeys is that male humans in every society provide for the females and their young. To be a man, therefore, carries with it not only the qualities mentioned above but the idea of responsibility." *Life* discusses as a contemporary problem that of man and woman in the conscious world forgetful of their unconscious selves, but literature has always pointed out as evil the failure of man-in-the-world to fulfill his archetypal role. The final stage in the resurrecting of each archetype, that of man and that of woman, demands sacrifice for others. Suffering is hard, but there is no dignity of the individual without it. Lord Jim, Raskolnikov, and Bazarov learn this truth reluctantly and surely.

One might make a point for Bazarov's death-bed shudder, making him more of a mock-Christ than a true Christ. So far as Bazarov himself *knows*, he may still be playing his nihilistic role. But Turgenev's tone, alternately comic and serious in its criticism of nihilism, suggests that Bazarov is better than he knows. He *does* direct others to understanding their defects and desires; he *does* help his father care for the serfs and dies because of it; and he *does* state finally to Anna the pathos of living without love and the tragic dignity of lives with love. The shudder of horror is the devil of Bazarov's intellect, but the heart and its blood have somehow made him a sacrificial hero.

BIBLIOGRAPHICAL NOTE:

JUNG AND ARCHETYPAL RELATIONSHIPS

Freud, Jung, and their lesser colleagues and disciples have a tremendous lot to say about the relationships within families and between generations. One should of course go to the original sources, but Patrick Mullahy in *Oedipus: Myth and Complex, a Review of Psychoanalytic Theory* (New York, 1955) points up the differences and the likenesses of the psychologists. Of special interest to our discussion at this point both as an approach and in content is Sigmund Freud's "Dostoyevsky and Parricide," *Partisan Review*, XIV (1945), pp. 530-544. Of more general and profound interest is Jung's essay on "Psychology and Literature" included in *Modern Man in Search of a Soul* (New York, 1934). Kerenyi and Jung's *Essays on a Science of Mythology: The Myth of the Divine Child and the Mysteries of Eleusis* (New York, 1949) relates in a fascinating way familial relationships and the pivotal myth of Demeter and Core. The famous application of Jung's archetypes to art is Maud Bodkin's *Archetypal Patterns in Poetry* (Oxford, 1934).

V

Christ As Artist And Lover:

D. H. LAWRENCE'S
Sons and Lovers

EVEN before the modern reader opens *Fathers and Sons*, the very title suggests the Freudian concept of the Oedipus complex. The inevitable conflict of father and son is of course implicit in the motif of the old champion versus the new champion, but not necessarily with the sexual emphasis of the Freudian approach. Even *Oedipus Rex*, which is literally sexual in its awful climax of revealed incest, derives its meaning from a vastly larger context of which the relationships of Oedipus and his mother are primarily symbols.

The sexuality of the unconscious as symbolism for primordial wishes rather than as literal repressed desires of the id brings to mind Jung instead of Freud. To Freud, the father is the great rival of his son. The son wants to be rid of him and regards the mother as his own. But the mores, which are always those of the father's milieu, teach the son guilt for his natural desires and indeed for the inevitability of his replacing the father. In these terms the writer of tragedy *is* conservative, for his final judgment and punishment of the son are according to the mores of the generation past. The mother develops into the grieving mother to lament what must, alas, be so.

Jung's restatement, and perhaps invalidation, of the Oedipus complex is more in line with the communal function and the traditional mode of tragedy. To Jung, the archetype of the mother is a loving, warming, nourishing, passively-creative, enduring concept. The archetype of the father is strong, authoritative, actively-creative. The son comes from both and needs both. As the child normally develops, the mother remains unconsciously and subtly the symbol of his compatibility with the context of life: nature, the family including his own wife and children, the environment of his neighbors and co-workers. The father becomes the symbol of the conscious contexts in which the son makes his way in the world, to which he pays homage, and for participation in which he receives praise: the society of men, socially and professionally; the dominant church; the current state. Jung puts it this way: "As the growing consciousness becomes more capable of understanding, the importance of the parental personality diminishes. But in the place of the father there comes the society of men, and in place of the mother, family and clan. Finally, instead of the father, the image of God appears, and in the mother's place, the mysterious abyss of all-being." To Jung, then, the "incest wish" is the impulse to recover the idyllic state of childhood protection by the parents; the dramatic expression of this wish as cohabitation with the mother is the desire to come into the mother once more to be born again. This unconscious wish to free ourselves from the complexities of domestic, occupational, and social involvements, which the growing man faces even before adulthood, is according to Jung the basis of most religious symbols, rites, and ceremonies. We want to purify ourselves, to recreate the lost Eden, to transcend the world, indeed to return to the great mother Earth and the great father Heaven.

As a matter of fact, *Fathers and Sons* involves little conflict in the Freudian sexual sense between Bazarov and his elders. In his insistence on the destruction of love and authority, he is at war with *both* parents. Herein is his nihilism, his irreligiosity. His return to them in spite of himself is for Jung figuratively incestuous, paradoxically with non-sexual connotations and basically spiritual in mood. Bazarov, we might say, is Freudian in *his* approach to himself and others: he might insist that he is out to kill his father just as he insists that Arkady and his infant half-brother will come to blows over their father's estate. Turgenev, on the other hand, is Jungian in *his* emphasis that the only true quest is for love. The tone of the novel—using tone traditionally as the attitude of the author toward his content—is as if Turgenev, Jung, were having a critical look at Bazarov, Freud.

Turgenev's story of fathers and sons, then, has little to do with sons and lovers in the sense that Lawrence later utilized the term as the title of his great novel. If one is reading Lawrence, the Freudian concept may be more fruitful, and we shall pursue it briefly as a way, one way, of looking at *Sons and Lovers*. I might reiterate at this point that I do not feel that one way of reading excludes another way. Every critic of whatever school is using his techniques to meet as fully as he can the demands of the author. He is applying his particular metaphor to the author's book and hoping to arrive at some

compatibility with the author's metaphor for experience.
Full compatibility is, alas, never possible, though the devoted adherents of particular schools of criticism may insist that their way is the only way to an ideal marriage
of critic and author.

To be sure, Lawrence's protagonist Paul is at war
with his father, Walter Morel, for the affection of his
mother, Gertrude. Even before Paul enters the story his
older brother William has replaced the father as the apple
of the mother's eye. When William dies, Lawrence
makes it clear that the closeness of Gertrude and Paul
evolves from the dramatic sacrifice of William.

Morel has been described as having once been a man
of tremendous vigor. When he and Gertrude met, he
was the epitome of masculinity with his "erect" phy-
sique, his "wavy black hair," his "vigorous black beard,"
his "ruddy" cheeks and "red, moist mouth," and his
"rich, ringing laugh." But Morel appears this way only
in summary; when the book begins, he has already lost
his position as man of the house. The financial lot of the
family has been hard. Morel has worked as a miner and
been shunted about by the bosses and the system. The
living conditions for him and his family have become
increasingly worse over the years: they have gradually
moved from the village of "Bestwood" through "Hell
Row" to "the Bottoms" as the "large mines of the finan-
ciers" replaced the small gin-pits and created the crowded
mining town as a part of their operations.

I might interject at this point that the Marxist critics
were once very much interested in Lawrence. In the literature section of John Strachey's *The Coming Struggle
for Power* Lawrence was one of several writers Strachey
chose to discuss. Lawrence, Mr. Strachey wrote,

was extremely interested, both consciously and unconsciously in class, and in class relationships. It would hardly
be too much to say that class relationships obsessed him.
For the same theme recurs over and over again in his novels.
A young, vigorous, unself-conscious worker is thrown into
governing class society and has a love affair with an aristocratic woman, who has up till then been unawakened
by the men of her own class. For example, *Aaron's Rod*
and *The Ghost*, one of his best short stories, contain this
theme: it appears again in his posthumous story *The Man
Who Died*, where his proletarian hero is by trade a carpenter [we shall mention this book below in quite a different context!]. And it is given its clearest expression in
that curious tract-like novel *Lady Chatterley's Lover*. In
this case, the governing-class husband is made actually, as
well as symbolically, impotent and crippled by the war.
The proletarian hero is always, of course, Lawrence himself.

Mr. Strachey's comment is obviously irrelevant to *Sons
and Lovers*, Lawrence's first and most famous novel. Of
course Lawrence's attitudes may have developed in the
direction that Mr. Strachey suggests, but even with respect to the examples he uses, his comments are superficial and at least in the case of *The Man Who Died* nonsensical. Still, there is one implication of his comment
which I consider worth pursuing, as we shall see presently. But back to Lawrence's picture of Morel.

In *Sons and Lovers* Gertrude Morel is hardly an
aristocrat, but she is a woman of an economic class above
that of Walter Morel, whose uninhibited masculinity
fascinated her and ended in their marriage. She is presented as small and delicate and "very intellectual," but
with hair as "bright as copper and gold, as red as burnt
copper," with "gold threads where the sun shines on it."

When the novel begins, one thinks almost immediately of Gertrude as a creature of the air and the sun somehow held in captivity by Morel in a kind of hell. Lawrence's imagery directly suggests this, as does the name Morel. Lawrence is probably employing the word *Morel* to suggest both of its common meanings: a kind of underground mushroom and a kind of sour and dark-colored cherry. Morel is a sort of broken Pluto of whose impotence the once Proserpine-like Gertrude partakes. The dramatic question is: who will rescue Gertrude from hell? She looks to her sons to do so, and they willingly accept the role of her rescuers from the life of death, of prince charmings who will reawaken the sleeping princess. Here is where Strachey's comment is relevant: he mentions stories in which the vigorous proletarian hero tries to "awaken" the woman married to an "actually, as well as symbolically, impotent and crippled" aristocrat. In *Sons and Lovers*, the proletarian husband is the monster who enslaves the sensitive wife. At first the role of savior is allotted to William, who betrays it by going to the city and succumbing to the temptations of love with a city girl (Strachey would have a good time with the Marxist approach here). Soon, however, after William dies (perhaps a figurative condemnation for his failure), Paul accepts the mission. We have, then, the artistic, intellectual young man as the would-be hero who will save the heroine, his mother, from the grossly physical and variously impotent monster, his father. The Freudian implications are striking.

Dramatically, however, the father is given little space. He is soon conquered by the closeness of the mother and the son with their common aesthetic sensitivity, and he finally disappears from the book almost entirely or enters the actual scenes apologetically and timidly. When the mother ultimately dies, it is as if the husband Morel is condescendingly allowed to be a grieving relative. Still, I do not have the impression that Paul, the son who replaces the father as the mother's lover and beloved, defeats the father through his own action. The delicate Gertrude is adept at fighting her own battles and has developed into a domineering woman impatient of her husband's defects and covetous of the role of both father and mother in the family situation. The outline of the "pure" Oedipus complex shifts to the consequent problem of the overprotective mother jealous of her son's attachment to other women and to the son's difficulty in making a normal sexual adjustment. Rather than the father and the son in battle over the mother, the center of the novel concerns primarily the mother and the girlfriends, Miriam and Clara, in battle over the son.

It has been facetiously suggested that in Lawrence's dramatic trinity, Paul is the son, Miriam is the holy ghost, and the mother is the father. More seriously, the physicality of the father, to which the sensitive Paul is opposed, becomes the materialism of the world in which he has to make his living. Here is the authority of the society with which Paul has to cope, and after this point he develops literally as the artist in conflict with an unartistic world. Miriam and the mother contest as to who is the inspiration for Paul's aesthetic expressiveness. It is difficult to determine who wins.

Before Paul is born, Lawrence has an impressive annunciation scene in which Mrs. Morel is given a sense of the specialness of the child which "boiled within her." In an argument with her drunken husband, she is shut outdoors in the summer night. There, "seared with passion," she shivers "to find herself out there in a great white light, that fell cold on her, and gave a shock to her inflamed soul." She walks to the strip of a garden which she has managed to maintain even in the Bottoms and stands there "in an immense gulf of white light, the moon streaming high in face of her, the moonlight standing up from the hills in front, and filling the valley where the Bottoms crouched, almost blindingly." Lawrence continues in the mystical vein as if she were the center of a unique fertility rite: she reels with the perfume of white lilies and dips her hand in the golden pollen of a white lily bin. "After a time the child, too, melted with her in the mixing-pot of moonlight, and she rested with the hills and lilies and houses, all swum together in a kind of swoon." After this ritual, never again is Walter Morel a part of the family: physically and psychologically his strength wanes until he is dramatically nothing after Paul is born. The very act of dipping her finger into the bowl of the flower is as if she has conceived Paul herself without any help from Morel. In any case, Paul never pays Morel homage as his father. Gertrude has achieved a kind of virgin birth in which she bears her own savior from the life of darkness with Morel.

Gertrude works to keep Paul close to her. She sympathizes with his trials in the world of business, and she encourages his painting, which baffles and bewilders his father. From her, says Lawrence, "he drew the life-warmth, the strength to produce; Miriam urged the warmth into intensity like a white light." The Madonna fights to keep the Son in her sphere. Miriam talks of "the Christian mystery" and wants a chaste, otherworldly relationship with Paul. Paul claims that his gift to Miriam is "as a mystic monk to a mystic nun." He cannot give to her completely and live in this our world. Mother and maiden contest over the devotion of a man.

But Paul is developing physically. As an artist he is a stranger to the world, he is what the virginal Miriam demands; but as a man, he must express his physicality. He demands intercourse with Miriam and makes out of it for himself a religion, but for her it is corruption and defeat. The aesthetic relationship with Miriam is replaced by the adulterous one with Clara. Oddly enough, Mrs. Morel could not endure Miriam's contest for his devotion, but she puts up with the affair with Clara, evidently sensing that it is not an affair of the spirit. Dramatically, Paul becomes free of his Oedipus complex, if one will. He is free of Miriam and of his approach to every woman as if she were the virginal mother, and he is free of the mother, who dies of cancer as the affair with Clara lingers on. Paul partakes in a kind of mercy-killing of the mother, glad for her that the pain is over and ambivalent in his feelings for himself. Clara returns to her husband, a worker in the world to which Paul does not really belong.

Alone, Paul faces Miriam again, but they can no longer communicate. What *did* she want of him: "did she want a Christ in him?" If so, he has been unable to fulfill her demands. "And what did he care that he wasted her? He had no religion." Lawrence uses words that are equally applicable to the mother, actually dead, and to Miriam, "feeling dead." He calls to his mother, but she has "intermingled herself" in the nature which to Paul *was* God. Paul is alone indeed, and he walks away to the "faintly humming, glowing town." In a sense, Paul, unable to be simply a soul for his mother and for Miriam and unable to be simply a body for Clara, has

become an individual in his own right. Christ and the
devil have combined to make a man.

I have intentionally tried to restate the narrative line
of *Sons and Lovers* in such a way as to suggest the inter-
relationship between a variety of approaches that might
be applied to the novel: the Freudian emphasis on basic
sexual relationships, the Jungian concept of archetypes,
the myth pattern of captured princess and rescuing
prince, the religious pattern of the immaculate birth of a
stranger to life. Each of these redescriptions can be supported by clusters of images without forcing the point in
question. In the context of this total discussion, reconsider
the religious pattern for a moment. I have described the
"immaculate conception" of Paul, the closeness of his
mother, and the exclusion of the father as one from the
lower depths. First the mother and then Miriam support
Paul in his fight with the physicality of the father and the
materialism of the world. Miriam, if one likes, simply vies
with Gertrude to be a virgin mother to Paul, but in another sense Gertrude wants to keep the son as her own in
this world but untouched by it and Miriam wants to lead
him into a kind of artistic otherworldliness. It is as if
Gertrude wants him to live the exemplary life, but live,
and as if Miriam has for him a higher calling than life itself. In any case, as Paul says, each in her own way
wants him to be Christ. But as Christ wears the guise of
man, so Paul falls into the physical relationship with
Clara, separating himself from the demands of Miriam
and the mother at once. Note that Paul's descent into the
world in his relationship with the unartistic, nonintense
Clara is literally taking on the flesh; Lawrence's details
are explicitly sexual. Finally, Paul is beaten up by Baxter

Dawes for his relationship with his wife Clara, for being a man, that is, but Paul forgives Baxter and helps to re-habilitate him from his shabby condition and to reunite him with his wife. It is after this point that Paul's mother dies and Paul disclaims the possibility of being Christ either to her or to her rival-substitute Miriam.

Lawrence's variation on the Christ pattern is, to be sure, highly sensual. It brings up such interesting questions as the relationship of the Oedipus myth to the Christ story on the one hand and of the concept of the Oedipus complex to both. To give Mr. Strachey his due, he finally kicks Lawrence out of the proletarian camp and accuses him of becoming "inextricably involved in that decline [of capitalist society]" and of escape into a "rather amateurish sort of sexual mysticism." Recall that Paul speaks derogatorily of Miriam's chatter about the "Christian mysteries" and claims that she wants to make a Christ of him. Miriam, however, accuses Paul of desir-ing "a sort of baptism of fire in passion," which she is unable to give him. Similarly, Clara cannot understand Paul's insistence that "the act of loving" is "the culmina-tion of everything," and Paul feels a "flash of hate" for her for not being able to understand. At another point, Miriam and Paul discuss religion. Miriam believes that "one should be religious in everything, have God, what-ever God might be, present in everything," but Paul in-sists that "God doesn't *know* things. He *is* things. And I'm sure He's not soulful." Miriam demands that he talk to her "through the spirit" rather than "through the senses," but Paul claims that "to be always beyond this mortal state would be to lose it," that married persons "live together as affectionate humans, who may be commonplace with each other without feeling awkward—not as two souls." The paradox is that Paul is insisting on the flesh but insisting on it in such an excruciating way that the flesh is for him the spirit. He may lament that he cannot be Christ in his abnegation of the flesh, and then his journey of learning may seem to be a mock-quest. But the women lament that they cannot reach the pedestal on which he places the flesh, and then he must remain alone as the stranger god to the less sensitive spirits of the world. Has Lawrence's tone reversed the dualism of the soul and the body? Is the transcendence of which ordinary mortals are incapable the complete expression of the physical-emotional self without the sterile, ascetic transcendence of orthodox Western religion? In the years to come, Lawrence suggested that it was.

If one studies the origins of religions, a point can be made for the natural bases of all rites and ceremonies. Christ is *the* spring god of our culture. Although formal Christianity frequently emphasizes in its rituals the wintry death which precedes his resurrection, a primordial sense that God is Love keeps forcing itself to the conscious level of words and celebrations. The rites of passage for Lawrence are maturation toward one's individual *manhood:* confirmation and bar mitzvah are occasions when Bazarov and Freud might warn the father to beware. But as the uncomplex Oedipus learns, the young man on two feet will become the old man on three, and there is a sacrament to remind us of that as well. The three-footed father is pushed into the background of the enveloping action of many of Lawrence's stories. His concern is rather with the rise from four feet to two. He writes usually of the first initiation, not of the final one. This may suggest a significant difference in stature between the confessional strain of "first" novels and the final, final mode of tragedy.

A late novel by Lawrence is *The Man Who Died*, which Strachey mentioned as a novel with a carpenter as proletarian hero (!). It is Lawrence's direct retelling of the Christ story. It points up clearly his ironic handling of the dualism of man and the god-in-man. The story is in two parts. The first part tells of a *man* who has been crucified, but who *physically* awakens from his unconscious state and in great pain leaves the tomb. He is met on the road by a peasant who takes him to his home and shelters him until he has recovered sufficiently to be on his way. The details of this part of the story that occur outside of the peasant's home carefully follow the pattern of the New Testament with Christ's after-death appearances, but Lawrence makes these actual rather than supernatural.

We shall pursue only a few of Lawrence's innumerable reinterpretations of the Biblical Christ story. To be sure, Lawrence treats his man's escape from the tomb as a rebirth, but in the figurative sense of a redefinition of attitudes. "The teacher and the saviour are dead in me," he says; "now I can go about my business, into my own single life." Lawrence makes a very telling point. He insists that the sense of having a mission in the world is a youthful feeling: "the man in him who had died . . . was . . . the man of his youth and his mission, of his chastity and his fear, of his little life, his giving without taking." It is obviously greedy to take without giving, but giving without taking is to Lawrence also a form of greed, of sterility. His man arises to the realization that "the body rises again to give and to take, to take and to give, ungreedily." He has been the betrayer in his insistence on a "public life," a "life of . . . self-importance," and he warns the woman Madeleine against following his mistake.

I keep thinking of "Theft," a fine story by Katherine Anne Porter. A young woman trying to be a writer in Greenwich Village comes to the realization that in the pursuit of fame she has stolen from herself the fulfillment of natural desires. In *Sons and Lovers* Lawrence is clearly concerned with the plight of the artist in society and with his lonely destiny. Every artist, in the sacrifices that he makes to preach his word, surely sees himself as a kind of self-denying god figure in relationship to an abusive society. This self-denial, interestingly enough, may have little to do with the flesh one way or another. The *complete* artist may demand fulfillment of his inclinations regardless of convention. On one level Lawrence keeps saying, as we shall see, that the mystery of sex is essential to fulfillment. The question may be whether Lawrence suggests that the "virginal" Christ with his mission was the wrong kind of artist or no artist at all or an artist without being a whole man.

One writer who treats the problems of the artist in society very literally is Thomas Mann in such stories as, say, "Death in Venice" and "Tonio Kröger." If I may, I shall interrupt my discussion of Lawrence to make a pertinent comment on Mann. Mann comes to the conclusion that the artist's destiny is lonely: his fate is to long for life but to be separated from it as he redeems through the word the bourgeois who deny him. As richly as any writer, Mann pursues the concept of the artist as "the stranger god," but he separates in the orthodox Nietzschean sense the kind of ascetic "stranger" that was Christ and the expressive "stranger" that was Dion-

ysus. For Mann the imitation of Dionysus is the abomination that fascinates and destroys the artist. For him art
is the *discipline* of feeling, the *objectification* of the life
that attracts. Ironically, this may turn out not to be the
case for Lawrence's artistic protagonists in his more
autobiographical stories. They always end up alone, dissatisfied with the artistic discipline of a Miriam and incompatible with the unartistic physicality of a Clara.
The problem of the artist as Mann states it and as Lawrence dramatizes it is how to maintain the golden mean
between the beauty of experience (Clara, the Platonic
matter) and the beauty of art (Miriam, the Platonic essence). In Mann the excessive pursuit of the former ends
in mortal death and of the latter in Death as the gate to
immortality. Perhaps Lawrence would interchange the
small letter and the capital.

Admittedly, the man with a youthful mission need
not be the literal artist. He could be the preacher, the reformer, the political leader—anyone who feels that he has
a mission to redeem man. The form that the mission
takes as far as the Christ-archetypes are concerned may
depend on the moment, or indeed on the unique combination of heredity and environment that goes into the
composition of any individual. In these terms, the dramatization of the artist in society, which the writer *always*
unconsciously treats, may take infinite shapes. Mann and
Lawrence are simply two writers who tend to treat the
theme consciously rather than vicariously.

One more point about the first half of Lawrence's
Christ story. His treatment of Christ as a *man* is full of
ironies, but it is hardly irreligious. He allows the Christ
figure a statement which includes all of the elements of
tragedy:

Now I can wait on life, and say nothing, and have no one betray me. I wanted to be greater than the limits of my hands and feet, so I brought betrayal on myself. And I know I wronged Judas, my poor Judas. For I have died, and now I know my own limits. Now I can live without striving to sway others any more. For my reach ends in my finger-tips, and my stride is no longer than the ends of my toes. Yet I would embrace multitudes, I who have never truly embraced even one. But Judas and the high priests saved me from my own salvation, and soon I can turn to my destiny like a bather in the sea at dawn, who has just come down to the shore alone.

The Greeks knew that tragedy had to be about man, not the god whose shape he imperfectly reflects. The writers of the New Testament perhaps knew this without knowing that they did. Or giving them their due, we might say that the so-called Christians who do not realize that Christ acts out for them the story of *man* may be missing the point.

What, then, does Lawrence do in the second half of *The Man Who Died* after bringing Christ to the tragic realization of his excesses? He sends Christ out of Israel to Lebanon. Here, in great pain from his wounds and with great fatigue from his journey, Christ seeks shelter for the night near a temple of Isis, which faces Egypt and "the splendid sun of winter." The priestess of the temple, the daughter of the woman who owns the plantation on which the temple is located, greets Christ as "the lost Osiris." At first Christ denies the identification, but the lure of the priestess and his own desire lead him to the temple where she worships.

Isis, to whom the temple is dedicated, has variously been identified with Aphrodite, the goddess of love, and

Demeter, the great earth mother. Her relation to Osiris, one of the famous Egyptian hero-gods, has been defined as wife, as sister, and as both at once. A series of stories, reminiscent of those of Dionysus and his variants (Adonis, Tammuz, Attis, etc.), describes the mutilation of Osiris, a principle of good, by his brother, Seth, a principle of evil, and his restoration to life by Isis, who had magical powers of healing. In some versions the mutilation of Osiris is specifically castration. In Egyptian mythology Osiris is the sacrificial hero whose death purifies mankind as do the deaths of Christ and Dionysus, and Isis is the female principle who gives continuity from death to resurrection, from death to resurrection for the male principle embodied in Osiris. The rites of Isis are sometimes associated with the Eleusinian mysteries of Demeter.

When Lawrence's priestess hails Christ as the lost Osiris, she is evidently playing the role of Isis restoring Osiris to the spring of life after the winter of his death. As pointed out, Christ at first resists the attempt at resurrection, but finally goes to the temple and accepts the ministry of the priestess. He walks naked with his wounds to the priestess before the statue of Isis. The priestess, one with Isis, chafes with oil the wounds of Christ, in her mind one with Osiris. "What was torn becomes a new flesh, what was a wound is full of fresh life," she chants and rubs. She kneels before the statue of Isis, and he approaches her:

He crouched to her, and he felt the blaze of his manhood and his power rise up in his loins, magnificent.

"I am risen!" he exclaims in a pun at once comic and serious.

Magnificent, blazing indomitable in the depths of his loins, his own sun dawned, and sent its fire running along his limbs, so that his face shone unconsciously.

Lawrence's Christ, in whom the youthful self of the public mission is dead, has risen through his individual being to the heights of a sun god. At the end of *The Man Who Died* the priestess of Isis, "full of the risen Osiris," is left with the child of Christ while the Christ figure leaves for whatever the morrow brings, possibly death now that he has at last lived.

Miriam accused Paul of demanding that sex be a "baptism of fire." Paul accused Miriam of demanding that he be a chaste Christ. Rising for Lawrence is ironically descent for the orthodox Christian of the Western world.

BIBLIOGRAPHICAL NOTE:

MARX, FREUD, AND FRAZER

I have chosen Strachey's *The Coming Struggle for Power* (New York, 1935) as a naïve example of Marxist criticism in its two highly readable chapters on literature, but there have been valuable and influential critics with implicit Marxist approaches. Among the truly exciting critics of our time are Christopher Caudwell: *Illusion and Reality* (London, 1937) and Kenneth Burke: *Attitudes towards History* (New York, 1937). There is indeed little that Kenneth Burke has not commented on interestingly and meaningfully. His essay on "Freud and the Analysis of Poetry" in *The Philosophy of Literary Form* (Baton Rouge, 1941) points out succinctly that the social and the psychological critics pay attention to different parts of a work and that one approach need not exclude another approach. Excellent examples of the Freudian and Marxist approaches respectively are Dr. Ernest Jones' *Hamlet and Oedipus* (Garden City, N. Y., 1954) and T. A. Jackson's *Charles Dickens: The Progress of a Radical* (New York, 1938). Needless to say, Lawrence's consciousness of sex teases one into Freudian readings that have their roots in such sections of Freud's *The Basic Writings* (New York, 1938) as "Wit and Its Relation to the Unconscious" and "Three Contributions to the Theory of Sex." Lawrence's approach in *The Man Who Died* reminds one of Édouard Schuré's *The Great Initiates: Sketch of the Secret History of Religions* (Paris, 1901; translated by Fred Rothwell, Philadelphia, 1922), which includes Christ with Rama, Krishna, Hermes, Moses, Orpheus, Pythagoras, and Plato; here Hermes is the Egyptian point of reference. The one-volume abridged edition of Sir James Frazer's *The Golden Bough* (New York, 1942) offers exciting reading in Chapters XXIX through XLIII on Adonis, Attis, Osiris, and Dionysus. Robert Graves' *The Greek Myths* (Baltimore, 1955) is a comprehensive compendiary of the traditional Greek narratives, their symbolic significance, and their relation to the myths of other cultures.

VI

Christ As Doomed Youth:

REMARQUE'S
All Quiet on the Western Front

LAWRENCE'S deification of the physical succeeded in shocking the orthodox thinkers of his time, and he was not averse to calling the world's attention to the fact that it should be shocked. In his famous essay on "Pornography and Obscenity," he had a passing word of praise for the amorality of post-World War I youth and a lengthy verbal spanking for the Victorians, who to his way of thinking had made sex filthy. One doubts if the youngsters who were so conscious of being "lost" could approach coitus as a "baptism of fire" any more than Miriam could—or more to the point here, the unintellectual Clara.

Lawrence's making a religion of the physical is a paradoxical development of the naturalistic tradition in fiction. In a sense, poor Emma Bovary asked no more or less than Paul Morel, and Flaubert effectively pointed out that she was questing death under the verbal guise of life, freedom, and transcendent love. The trouble may be that Emma imitated the artists without the capacity to be an artist; she was not sufficiently a stranger to life to find in life more than the prosaic. Like Paul, she tended to talk about "God in everything," but unlike Paul, she did not feel it.

What would Conrad and Dostoyevsky and Turgenev have said about Lawrence's brand of mysticism? When Lawrence's Christ experienced in his loins, "I am risen!" would Conrad have said, "the liver, not the soul"? The old question of where the seat of the soul is, comes up: in the brain, in the heart, between the legs, or the indefinable "something else besides" located, to be sure, everywhere and nowhere? Perhaps it is a matter of tone— my gross "between the legs" is hardly Lawrence's "magnificent, blazing indomitable in the depths of his loins." Conrad may have accepted the reverence in Lawrence's attitude despite the extreme physicality of his imagery and, indeed, theme. Miriam and Sonia are both like burning white lights, but Dostoyevsky's drama moves us toward Sonia and Lawrence's away from Miriam. Lawrence in effect invalidates the orthodox dualistic approach to man, for in him the body is the end *and* the beginning. It is hardly the nature of man for which penance must be done.

Lawrence's immersion in the physical, as we have suggested, is an ironic outgrowth of the nihilistic naturalism of which Bazarov, for example, was guilty. According to the tone of Turgenev, the naturalistic, deterministic, monistic climate of the nineteenth century was pathetic by its very nature. He accused it of having forgotten the eternal verities validated by the truth of experience, not by the testings of science. In this same naturalistic climate Lawrence somehow found these verities. As much as it was the Victorians, was it the naturalistic writers themselves—Flaubert, Zola, Norris, Dreiser—who presented man's very physicality as his pathetic plight? Lawrence would not have it so: contrast the tone implicit, say, in Epstein's famous statue of Adam with, again, Lawrence's "I am risen!"

Most of the writers of the first two decades of this century were concerned more with man's imprisonment in a social cage rather than in the cage of the flesh. If the latter to Lawrence was no cage at all, the former was frequently implicit in the enveloping action which he created for his characters. The Marxist critic, we have seen, tended to make the social pathos all important in the early Lawrence, but actually such emphasis was never major in his works. Lawrence's Christ, when he was young, had a reforming zeal to save the world, but the concern with the public mission was defined as death itself. *The Man Who Died* can be read on one level as Lawrence's saying to his contemporaries that social consciousness is part of a *mock*-quest. Dostoyevsky would have agreed on that much, but the point of body-consciousness at which Lawrence arrived he might have restated as the irreligious, physical hedonism of his satanic Svidrigailov.

The pathos of the naturalistic approach, from which Lawrence's worship of the body ironically freed him, was accentuated for the slightly younger writers by the experience of World War I. The poetry of Wilfred Owen, the remarkably talented young Englishman who died in France in 1918, a week before the Armistice, contained within its few lines most of the attitudes which the post-war novelists were to express in recollection. He contrasted the reality of death to the illusions of the society at home: if you could see war, he told the generation which had reared and educated him,

> you would not tell with such high zest
> To children ardent for some desperate glory,
> The old lie: *Dulce et decorum est*
> *Pro patria mori.*

He pointed up the ironies of youth caught in a plight it
did not make and did not understand. "What passing-
bells for these who die as cattle?" he asked rhetorically,
but proceeded to give an answer that inverted traditional
religious imagery and reduced it to a mockery:

> Only the monstrous anger of the guns.
> Only the stuttering rifles' rapid rattle
> Can patter out their hasty orisons.

The attack on the lies by which we live, the comparison
of men to trapped animals, the ironic juxtaposition of the
words of resurrection and the experience of final death
were all characteristic of the nineteenth-century naturalism which so disturbed Dostoyevsky, Turgenev, and
Conrad. Furthermore, they continued to be characteristic of the new writing well through the 1920's.

Still, something about the tone and mood of Owen
was not completely without hope and consolation, and
this elusive positiveness sometimes breaks through the
pathos and dominates the poetry. It was inevitable that
writers compared young men dying in war to Christ as
the crucified innocent, and Owen repeatedly did so directly and implicitly. In some poems, the tone was anger
at the crucifiers (not the enemy, but the older generation
of one's own parents and leaders), and these were without consolation in the face of death. But in other poems,
though the world was rejected as lost morally and the
young soldiers described as lost physically, there is a

groping to express the transcendent beauty of the untouched innocents on the battlefield.

> Heart, you were never hot,
> Nor large, nor full like hearts made great with shot;
> And though your hand be pale,
> Paler are all which trail
> Your cross through flame and hail:
> Weep, you may weep, for you may touch them not.

Or in still another poem, a Christ-like figure met in a dream identifies himself:

> I am the enemy you killed, my friend,

and forgivingly accepts his murderers into the company of those who, when the time comes, will rise to cleanse the chariot wheels of the world of the blood which will clog them till they can no longer turn. In a final version of this poem, the Christ-figure speaks to the young soldier:

> Beauty is yours and you have mastery,
> Wisdom is mine, and I have mystery.

An aura of tenderness and belief is in constant conflict with anger and pathetic resignation. The latter, again, is frequently revealed through mock-religious imagery and the former through the serious use of Christ as a correlative.

Remarque's *All Quiet on the Western Front*, completed ten years after Owen's death, achieves a similar paradox of softness in the midst of harshness. In this sense it is strikingly different from the number of war novels that are basically stories of the development of youth from naïve commitment to experienced detachment. Hemingway's *A Farewell to Arms*, a great novel on many levels, is an example of the initiation story in which the innocent in the modern world learns that he is vulnerable to hurt by an indifferent universe and that the length of his survival depends on deliberate protection against vulnerability. To be sure, Hemingway's characters are always questing love, a home, religion, order, but they do not find them because they are unwilling to admit that suffering and sacrifice are essential to achieved commitment. The structure of the book is tight: a step by step journey from innocence to experience. And the style is economic in keeping with the theme of the advisability of hiding the emotions from a world which will torture them.

All Quiet makes basically the same points as *A Farewell to Arms*, but its methods are totally unlike Hemingway's and its mood is different. Remarque's constant refrain is literally: "We are a lost generation," we who were too young to have roots in experience and who have discovered that the words intended as roots by parents, teachers, preachers, politicians have no relationship to experience. Remarque's hero is nineteen when the book begins and twenty when he dies, and he has a strong feeling that even the men of twenty-five who have wives and children of their own have a sense of something to return to. In one scene the soldiers typically discuss what they will do when the peace comes, but with a sense that the young men dragged out of school into war have had no chance even to create the lies by which men live in peacetime. Now, facing the truth of death so soon, they are denied the years of illusion which are the luxury of living before every man faces the heart of darkness and makes his individual adjustment to it.

Remarque's protagonist Paul, who tells his own story, is constantly surprised that at the age of nineteen he has, as Hemingway might put it, "lived with death a long time." According to Paul, his journey of learning was practically completed in his "first bombardment." In that moment, "the world as they [the older generation] taught it to us broke in pieces . . . we saw that there was nothing of their world left. We were all at once terribly alone; and alone we must see it through." For the archetypal sacrificial heroes, death and the aloneness with which one faces it come at the end of the epic drama, but Paul in effect begins with them. This consciousness of the shocking shortening of the journey of learning is forever with us in the novel. It is in every episode, and it is in image after image. In a day a child moves from innocence to experience. In a year a young man moves from maturity to death. At the climax of the novel Paul moves across a foxhole to a French soldier whom he has killed because he had to:

I drag myself toward him, hesitate, support myself on my hands, creep a bit farther, wait, again a terrible journey of three yards, a long, a terrible journey.

This is the most telling image of the book, "a terrible journey of three yards," a life shortened in space as throughout the novel it is shortened in time.

Here is indeed the essence of art. Selection, the symbolic short cut, careful manipulation of structure allow us to live a lifetime in two hours in the theater or through thirty pages or a thousand in fiction. It is literally time and space that are shortened for us so that we suspend our disbelief and accept the eternal and the universal which endure beyond all time and space. In these terms,

Greek tragedy is perhaps the epitome of art in that it
juxtaposes the vastest of themes with the greatest limitations of time and space. There is something here subtly
akin to the essential pun that we mentioned before:
timelessness is effectively proclaimed in a short time! At
the beginning of the play, Oedipus seems to be on two
feet. The attaining of his lofty position even from birth
is traced for us in summary after summary: the very
technique of the delved-out memory is essential to the
central narrative. Before the day is done Oedipus has
moved from innocence and pride to experience and humility. He leaves the stage virile and kingly in appearance, though aged now in spirit, and returns suddenly
and shockingly a broken old man, the guise of the flesh
compatible with the state of the soul. As if this were not
enough, now old, he is for the first time truly young;
now blind, he at last sees. All of this literally and artistically in less than an hour!

But the overall method of Remarque that reflects his
dominant image of the journey of life in an infinitesimal
context of space and time is more romantic than classical.
The classical writer tells a story clearly and surely step
by step, from exposition through separable steps of the
complication up to a climax and into a denouement. He
creates a readily outlined narrative, reducing the over-
whelmingly general to the excruciatingly sharp specific.
He creates drama in the traditional sense of the word:
ideas and judgments are implicit in the overt action of his
characters. Let us put it this way: the method of the
classicist is logical and chronological though his theme
may be the irrationality of rational man and the absurdity of time. On the other hand, the romantic story-teller
has constantly groped for a method that has a less ironic

and a more literal relationship to the emotional nature of man and the smallness of time and space. Sterne, Proust, Joyce, Virginia Woolf have all tried to free their stories of man from order as indeed, to their way of thinking, man is truly freed from it. Their methods are associative rather than logical, psychological rather than chrono-logical. Another way of putting it: more lyric than narra-tive, more poetic than prose-like.

All Quiet achieves its disregard of time through a kind of lyric method. Paul, the protagonist, tells his story in an almost impressionistic manner. He moves back and forth in time from the present moment to past moments as details of the present suggest episodes of the past to him. He moves between the description of action and the lyrical expression of feelings and evaluations. The events that evolve *can* be placed in time and space, but this is not important: the effect is lyrical and tender, not epic and grand, the emotional expression of a moment to which a lifetime has been reduced. In structure, as in that of so many first novels, *All Quiet* seems loose, unpolished, youthful, but it *is* youthful and therein is both its failure and its success as art.

In one passage of the kind of lyricism to which I refer, Paul is speaking:

It is chilly. I am on sentry and stare into the darkness. My strength is exhausted as always after an attack, and so it is hard for me to be alone with my thoughts. They are not properly thoughts; they are memories which in my weakness turn homeward and strangely move me.

The parachute-lights shoot upwards—and I see a pic-ture, a summer evening. I am in a cathedral cloister and look at the tall rose trees that bloom in the middle of the little cloister garden where the monks lie buried. Around the walls are the stone carvings of the Stations of the Cross. No one is there. A great quietness rules in this blossoming quadrangle, the sun lies warm on the heavy grey stones. I place my hand upon them and feel the warmth. At the right-hand corner the green cathedral spire ascends into the pale blue sky of the evening. Between the glowing columns of the cloister is the cool darkness that only churches have, and I stand there and wonder whether, when I am twenty, I shall have experienced the bewildering emotions of love.

The image is alarmingly near; it touches me before it dissolves in the light of the next star-shell.

The Stations of the Cross is a correlative to which the reader responds intuitively, and I respond to it deliberately as well in terms of the Christ-motif in which I have been interested. For the moment, follow these responses, the intuitive and the deliberate one, and see where they lead us. When we come across the direct reference to Christ, we think with a feeling akin to *pieta* of the plight of Paul and the other young men being sacrificed in the war. We may think too of the young men bearing the cross for an entire society which with good or bad intentions has condemned them to die. We think, in this passage at least, of death as a way to life, for the imagery of the passage is that of growth and regeneration: rose trees blooming in the night, a "blossoming quadrangle" of stone still warm with the day's sun, a green spire reaching upward into a blue sky. Or we may think on the other hand of a kind of lost Eden for which Paul longs in a world of death. In the paragraph which follows, Paul himself describes the memory as a "calm" one, but a calmness against which he must protect himself lest he drop his defenses against the ever-lasting "unquietness" of the front.

Or more deliberately: The Stations of the Cross which Paul recalls having seen in a cathedral garden were the pictorial representations, sometimes in painting, sometimes as here in bas-relief, of Christ's "journey" from his condemnation to death up to the point at which his body was laid in the tomb. Church lore differs as to how many "stations" there actually were, but most representations suggest the following fourteen: (1) Christ is condemned to death; (2) the cross is laid upon him; (3) he falls for the first time; (4) he meets his Blessed Mother; (5) Simon of Cyrene is made to bear the cross; (6) Christ's face is wiped by Veronica; (7) he falls for the second time; (8) he meets the women of Jerusalem; (9) he falls for the third time; (10) he is stripped of his garments; (11) he is crucified; (12) he dies on the cross; (13) his body is taken down from the cross; (14) his body is laid in the tomb. In the Middle Ages a definite ritual developed around these picturizations whereby the devotee went in effect on a miniature vicarious pilgrimage along the way Christ traversed in Jerusalem from Pilate's house to Mount Calvary. The more fortunate devout of course actually made the trip to Jerusalem and traversed in person the "Via Dolorosa," as the way of the cross became known.

Remarque's reader soon thinks of the way of the cross again, for on the very next page Paul says that the way of those who have roots is the way of nostalgia, but for himself and the other lost ones, "these memories of former times do not awaken desire so much as sorrow—a strange, apprehensible melancholy." The way of his generation, like the way of Christ bearing the cross, *is* the way of sorrow. The very imagery of the journey is with us once more:

Today we could pass through the scenes of our youth like travellers. . . . We long to be there; but could we live there?
We are forlorn like children, and experienced like old men, we are crude and sorrowful and superficial—I believe we are lost.

Paul's journey, then, like Christ's, is the "via dolorosa," the way from the condemnation to death, to the actual death on the last page of the novel. This is not as far as we can deliberately go with the image, the Stations of the Cross. It would be an interesting piece of crafts-manship if, say, the steps of Paul's journey to his death were symbolically those of Christ, in the same way that the twelve central adventures of Joyce's Stephen follow the divisions of the *Odyssey*, but in this book Remarque is not that kind of a writer. Having taken the Stations of the Cross as a correlative, one might relate the gambling for Christ's garments to Remarque's motif of: Who will get the dead man's shoes? The removing of the shoes from the dying is an age-old folk motif that can be read on as many levels as, say, Oedipus, and in some versions its implications are not unlike those of the soldiers' desiring Christ's robe without respect for his death. But in *All Quiet* the claiming of the clothes of the dead men is not part of any structure analogous to the traditional structure of Christ's Stations. Remarque's structure, as we have said, is more lyrical and associative than narra-tive and logical.

The Stations of the Cross, then, is a dominant image at a pivotal point, but neither a key to overall structure nor a part of any cluster of images more specific than the broad sacrificial-hero ones. We have mentioned before a possible difference between integrated meanings and parallel ones. The difference is not always valid, but pursuit of the parallel as if it were an integral part of the whole quickly points up the precariously parasitic and absurd nature of literary criticism. I admit my own tendency toward critical venturing. In the light of my own interest in the Christ patterns of the novels in which I had at first *intuitively* discovered them, I *did* look up Stations of the Cross. The sources which I read with interest listed the "stations" or steps in Christ's final journey to death in much the same way as I have above and besides discussed the derivation of the word *station*. A *station*, according to one source, is a fast of bread and water, whereby as pilgrims we simulate the suffering of Christ. Even in this sense, it may come from a military metaphor that occurs several times in the Bible as, for example, in ". . . we are also God's soldiers," the Latin word for soldier or military guard having been *statio*. Ah, I said, *station . . . soldier . . . also God's soldiers . . .* Remarque's soldier Paul. Another source referred station more directly to *stationarius*, "a military encampment," and then figuratively, "an encampment protecting one from the assaults of the devil." Again, *station . . .* the place in which we *stand* to repel the enemy . . . the manifold irony that the word *enemy* has taken on by Remarque's last page. True, creative writing demands creative reading, but the obligation of the reader is to be imaginative *within* the limits of the book. Parallels are interesting and enlightening, but pursuing them is like playing a game for which there are no rules: it's both too easy and too hard.

One is tempted to play a similar game with the name Paul. In *Sons and Lovers*, for example, where some of the names are obviously symbolic, the protagonist Paul is called by his intimates " 'Postle," teasing the reader to consider the associations of the Biblical name. The Biblical Paul was martyred for his letters. He felt himself free of the conventional law, for the true law was in the mystic union of the believer with the crucified Lord. He emphasized the purity of family life. He preached fellowship not only with Christ but with fellow-believers. Is Lawrence pointing to any one of these associations, or all of them, or none? Does an awareness of the apostle Paul's literary martyrdom enrich Lawrence's motif of the artist and the society? Perhaps this much at least. And what of Remarque's Paul? Does an awareness of the Biblical Paul's preaching of fellowship enrich young Paul's refrain that the "finest thing that arose out of the war" was "comradeship"? Coincidentally and significantly, yes, but hardly because Remarque was using the name Paul as a guide to meaning.

Comradeship in the face of death is essentially a religious idea, and Remarque handles it as such throughout his novel. Communion as a kind of holy eating together by way of transcending the death to which men are damned is a dominant image of the book. There is a wonderful scene in which Paul and Kat, the older man who serves as a kind of natural mentor to Paul and his group, eat a goose they have stolen in a previous comic episode. They eat, and two men who "formerly . . . should not have had a single thought in common . . . sit with a goose between us and feel in unison, and are so intimate that we do not even speak. . . . I love him. . . . We are brothers and press on one another the

choicest pieces." Later, in a deserted village to which
Paul, Kat, and others are assigned, there is a long, happy
last eating scene before Paul is wounded. In the last narrative action of the book Paul carries the wounded Kat
back to the post. On the way Paul thinks that Kat has
fainted, but when he arrives, he discovers that his burden
has been hit in the head with a splinter. Paul has saved
Kat only to have him die. An orderly, noticing Paul's
stunned response, asks: "You are not related, are you?"
"No, we are not related. No, we are not related," Paul
thinks with all of the ironic awareness that every man
is related to every other man. This Paul like the other
one preached fellowship with those in the same plight
with himself.

If all men are brothers, who then is the enemy?
Paul looks at Russian prisoners through a barbed wire
fence. He knows that the very "word of command"
which has made them enemies can transform them into
friends. He is frightened, for to think in that way lies
"the abyss." If he is to survive, he must repress these
thoughts until after the war has ended. Then, perhaps,
pursuing them, he might give purpose to his questless
life. Paul breaks his cigarettes in half and shares them
with the Russians; he gives them part of the cakes his
mother has made for him.

The scene with the Russians is preparation for the
climax of the book which we have already mentioned in
another connection. Paul, lost from his patrol, is hiding
in a fox hole. He stabs a retreating Frenchman who
falls into the hole beside him. Watching him die, Paul at
last makes the "terrible journey" of three yards across
the bottom of the hole till he is beside his victim. By
three o'clock the man is dead. After all, Paul's matura-

tion turns out not to have been completed in that first bombardment. Never before has he seen a man die whom he, Paul, has killed with his own hands. Throughout the book Paul and his friends have blamed worldwide diplomats, the Kaiser, the generals, the manufacturers, the parents, the preachers, the teachers for their plight in the war, but now Paul takes responsibility for the sins of man in which he has participated. "Forgive me, comrade; how could you be my enemy? If we threw away these rifles and this uniform you could be my brother just like Kat." Paul swears a life of penance and sacrifice for the death of the man whose life has been bound up in some mysterious way with his own life. He promises to devote himself after the war to helping his "enemy's" family. He has crucified a stranger, and he *will* suffer for this greatest of all sins.

But back in the trenches with his own men, he is reassured and comforted. "After all, war is war." Business is business, and life is life. This is the conscious world where the devil rules. To deny it, that is, to pursue the godhead, is martyrdom on behalf of one's brothers. That way lies "the abyss," according to convention and the devil. But according to the godhead which Paul would imitate if he could, that way is salvation. What Paul learns in his journey for a moment and for all time is that man cannot pursue the truth and live. Of course, as Hemingway says, if he does not pursue it, he dies too, but only a little later. The joker is that the early death in the cause of truth may be the one way to the everlasting life.

BIBLIOGRAPHICAL NOTE:

THE STORY AS JOURNEY *○ ⁄ₙ ₐ⌐*

The Stations of the Cross are described meticulously and interestingly under "The Way of the Cross," *The Catholic Encyclopedia* (New York, 1910) and under "Stations," *Encyclopedia of Religion and Ethics* (New York, 1928). The concept of *journey* as a figurative way of describing learning *and* of pointing to the literal and thematic structure of story telling is closely related to such psychological works as Jung's *Psychological Types or the Psychology of Individuation* (New York, 1926) and such exciting studies of myth as Joseph Campbell's *The Hero with a Thousand Faces* (New York, 1945). The psychologist's concern with *development* or *maturation* even in a fundamental psychology text, the anthropologist's concern with *rites of passage* or *initiation* even in a summary discussion of primitive cultures, and the literary critic's concern with *structure* in indeed the most conventional approach to literature, all encourage the use of a controlling image such as *journey*.

VII

Christ As The Missing Orient:

FITZGERALD'S
The Great Gatsby

BOTH *Heart of
Darkness* and *Lord Jim* achieve their dramatic structure
more through the step-by-step learning processes of
Marlow than from any traditionally organized revelation of Kurtz or of Jim himself. Whether Conrad is
writing in the third person or having Marlow repeat
his discoveries in the first person, the effect is that of the
Jamesian "central intelligence," so characteristic of the
great late nineteenth-century novels and so influential on
the great twentieth-century ones. In this method everything is seen by or through the eyes of Marlow. Nevertheless, the author allows us by his skillful manipulation
of tone to objectify the responses of Marlow and to
judge him as fully as the character whom he himself is
attempting to judge.

This method is a facet of the subjectivity which generally characterizes the style of Conrad. Ironically, it also
characterizes the style of many post-World War I writers
considered naturalistic in their content or economical and
objective in their technique. Again, Hemingway is the

conspicuous example. It used to be critical routine to describe Hemingway's method as the scientific, reportorial style at which the naturalists aimed but which they rarely achieved. A simplicity of diction: short words at a low level of abstraction. The elementary structure of sentences: simple sentences and run-on sentences. The infrequency or near-absence of figures of speech: a few comparisons, but rarely a figurative one. The restraint of tone: persistent understatement. But Hemingway's impressive use of the first-person narrator and the third-person central intelligence gives his books and stories a highly subjective kind of unity. For example, he has Lieutenant Henry tell his own story in *A Farewell to Arms* and usually tells the story of Nick Adams in the third person though his focus of narration is Nick himself. In the case of Conrad, the very method of writing reflects the theme of "haze" instead of the specific "kernel," the "soul" instead of the "liver," the "something else besides" instead of the "fact." Hemingway's methods are distinctly different from Conrad's, but to be sure they appropriately symbolize *his* early themes. Complex sentences functionally designate the logical relationship of things, and Hemingway's comparative lack of them implies that nature is chaotic, uncontrollable by any so-called rational man. In the traditional complex sentence one thing (the independent clause) is more important than another (the dependent clause) in a particular way (casual, temporal, concessive, etc.). But for Hemingway an attempt at ordering and relating the parts of nature is unrealistic, like the unattainable world of the Abruzzi where peasants tip their hats to you and call you "sir" or like Catherine Barkley's early lesson that everything has an explanation. All that man can do is to accept the impact of the world around him in a series of separate stimuli which play upon him—in separate simple sentences, or in run-on sentences of separate things joined by *and*, or in a vocabulary characterized by nouns and by adjectives that are descriptive rather than evaluative. At the most, he can put off the hurt of this impact by avoiding the involvements of belief and love: hence the understatement, which ironically points up that belief and love are what men want. The very style reflects the defenses which helpless man temporarily builds up against the dangers of attachment and the inevitable loss in the indifferent world around him. But since man wants to believe and to love and be loved, he pathetically falls into the trap of attachment. Then Hemingway overflows into an excited impressionism of style, foreshadowing the tremendous hurt that his character will feel when the world attacks his momentarily unfortified self. In *A Farewell to Arms*, for example, when Henry is either drunk or making love, the number of run-on sentences increases and the length of the independent clauses within them decreases. This results in a heightened pace, a rapid flow of thoughts and feelings. In these sections, the movement from one kind of subject matter to another is conspicuously associative rather than logical or chronological, and transitions depend on the repetition of a noun rather than on traditional connecting words that point up how the next thought logically derives from the preceding one. This style, by conventional designation, is what we would call impressionistic. Incidentally, it reveals clearly the close relationship between the method of Hemingway and that of Gertrude Stein, from whom he supposedly learned much. Interestingly enough, the impressionistic passages, in which the character's defenses against emotions are dropped, are primarily an accentuation of the method of the seemingly detached, understated sections. Hemingway's detachment, then, is not the imposition of reason upon the emotions (not, that is, syntax); it is a kind of dead-pan *subjectivity*, as I try to show below. Finally, the emotional hurt, prepared for by the impressionistic outbursts, returns Hemingway's protagonist predictably to an increased restraint of feeling and Hemingway to an increased flatness of style, which makes the unsophisticated reader ask at the end of stories, "So what?"

The effect of Hemingway's style is admittedly about as different from that of Conrad's as it can possibly be, but my point is that it is no less subjective, really. Conrad's narrator Marlow and Hemingway's central intelligence, say, Henry or Nick, have simply opposing things to learn. Appropriately, the very things they are learning come through in the style of the books even before the characters have insight enough to put their lessons into words. The author knows the answers already, and this of course results in the irony that allows the reader to stand somehow outside of the very character through whom the entire story is being told. Marlow has to learn the mystical nature of man that saves him from himself and the world; Henry, already a "tough" soldier, has to relearn the defenselessness into which emotional attachments lead. But, in both, the styles from the beginning tell the reader what the world demands of men, whether it be Conrad's belief or Hemingway's detachment.

The lessons are different, but the employment of a central intelligence directs us to find structure in a story through the step-by-step education of the focus of nar-

ration about the nature of things. The modern story
which gets its unity from this method attains meaning
primarily as a journey of learning for the narrating intelligence, though the reader may be distracted to looking for structure in the character from whom the lesson
is learned. Kurtz, then, is the sensational center of *Heart
of Darkness*, but Marlow's development through Kurtz
is the structural and thematic center of the story. Kurtz,
dramatically speaking, hardly develops; he is the accomplished example from whom Marlow learns encour-
agingly the dualistic nature of man.

The now almost classic example of the learning
story is Hemingway's "The Killers," which turns out
not to be concerned with the killers primarily or even
with Ole Andreson, to whom the movie version, like the
conventional reader, directed its attention. Its structural
and thematic center is Nick Adams, who learns in several
well-executed steps that the world is not what he has
been brought up to expect. In direct contrast to Marlow,
Nick may learn in this and other stories man's lack of
freedom. But again, my emphasis is that both Conrad's
Heart of Darkness and Hemingway's "The Killers" are
stories of learning, of growing up, of the coming of
age for the narrators rather than the more traditional
stories of character revelation or even naturalistic slices-
of-life. Nick's discussion with Ole Andreson is like a
kind of negative catechism, recalling Catherine's nostalgic statement that she had been brought up to believe
that everything had an explanation. He has been faced
with the shocking amorality of the killers who are mur-
dering a man they don't even know, much less feel intensely about; with his own lack of physical freedom;
with chance involvement; with Sam's defeatist attitude

toward evil. And now in Ole Andreson he is faced with the pathos of a man resigned to his petty destiny. First, he suggests as a way out an appeal to the order of society: "Don't you want to go and see the police?" Second, his own individual action: "Isn't there something I could do?" Third, a romantic refusal to see the situation for what it is: "Maybe it was just a bluff." Fourth, the just as romantic escape from problems by going elsewhere: "Couldn't you get out of town?"—certainly a meaning-ful question for Hemingway, the expatriate. And finally even appeal to the gangster's code, showing how almost insidiously Nick is being taught the force of evil: "Couldn't you fix it up some way?" The other unhappy lessons of the story are manifold. As Nick's final emo-tional statement "It's too damned awful" suggests, he has other lessons to learn in a whole series of stories yet to come chronologically in his experience.

Marlow, acquiring one of his first jobs in *Heart of Darkness*, is also the innocent setting out in the world. He meets evil, yes, in his recognition of the jungle that is as much in Europe as in Africa, and in a highly sig-nificant scene he almost meets death: "they very nearly buried me." Still, he survives for "affirmation" and "moral victory" and for the retelling of Kurtz's and his own story "in the pose of a meditating Buddha." He has figuratively been on a quest and successfully faced the "heart of darkness" and transcended it. It is as if he were a grail knight overcoming the dread sight of the perilous jungle and restoring meaning to a dead life. Nick, whether he knows it or not (and often the grail knight does not), is also on a quest, but repeatedly he sees evil without being able to remedy it or receives wounds without hope of being healed. Hemingway's continual use of the wound as the symbol for the hurt which the world imposes upon man, makes one constantly wish for the medicine man who played such an important part in the nature cults out of which, reputedly, the grail legends developed. In "Big Two-Hearted River," which I mention in another connection below, Nick Adams returns home (presumably from the war) wounded and tired, finds the previously wooded area of his homeland largely burned out, goes through rituals in which he tries to recapture the nature of his youth, and attempts unsuccessfully to catch a big fish. It is surprising how many elements of the grail pattern are actually present in the Nick stories: the innocent passing through the trials of a world, the waste land, the wounded knight, the fish as a symbol of life—in a mixed-up sort of way since the questing knight, the wounded knight, and the Fisher King are all combined in one figure here. There is this same cluster of grail images, with a similar fusing of separate elements, in *The Sun Also Rises*, where the wound of the protagonist Jake Barnes is specifically the impotency of the traditional Fisher King.

As to what comes first—the use of a central intelligence, the theme of discovery of the self and the world, the quest pattern, or the objective correlative of the grail story—is a chicken-and-egg question. One might quite convincingly contend that the writers of the 'twenties who were concerned, again in contrast to Conrad, with the *futile* search for faith and love, acquired their ironic grail references second-hand from T. S. Eliot, who in turn borrowed most of his from Miss Jessie Weston's *From Ritual to Romance*. Eliot's *The Waste Land* has turned out to have a tremendous influence on writers since 1922, the date of its publication. It became the handbook of despair for an entire decade of writers, just as Eliot has since become the symbol of belief for our decade.

At the risk of repeating details of which the reader is already aware I should like to recall several separate elements of *The Waste Land* pertinent to my purposes. The title comes from the ancient legend of the Holy Grail, which may be roughly restated as follows: A monarch known as the Fisher King has been mysteriously wounded in the genitals, and the land over which he rules has become arid and barren, in effect a waste land. The king will be reinvigorated and the land will become productive again when a knight, strong in body and pure in heart, arrives to attend the hurt ruler. The knight, in his process of saving the king, must go through many trials in order to reach the Chapel Perilous in the center of the waste land. There he must endure his most frightening ordeals, involving darkness and the supernatural and death itself. If he overcomes these obstacles successfully, he goes on to secure the castle and heal the king, thereby restoring faith and productivity to the people and the land. A step in the final salvation may include, too, the rescuing of a miraculous cup or dish and the repairing or recovering of a broken or useless lance.

According to Miss Weston and other students of the grail legend, the grail romances with which we are most familiar, the stories involving Gawain or Galahad or Percival as seekers of the grail, derived from ancient nature cults celebrating simultaneously the wonders of the cycle of the seasons and the reproduction and continuation of human beings. In the rituals of these cults

various personifications of sun and spring gods, such as
Tammuz, Attis, Adonis, Mithra, were celebrated as the
bringers of light to darkness, of warmth to cold, of
growth to barrenness, of spring to winter, of birth to
death, both physically and spiritually. The cup and the
lance which figured in them were originally sexual symbols of the female and male in the union which brought
birth. Over the centuries, new cults borrowed from already established cults out of which they had developed
or with which they had come into contact directly or by
folk tradition. Or peoples having the same needs and
partaking of the same natural processes dramatized their
feelings similarly.

The step from Mithra to Christ, for example, is
easy enough, and though the early Christians may have
frowned on the mysteries of other cults, they frequently
borrowed from them or changed them, both for their
own purposes and for the attraction of native peoples.
The female symbol of the cup, for instance, became trans-
formed into the cup out of which Christ drank at the
Last Supper and which, consequently, figures so im-
portantly in the ritual of communion. The phallic symbol of the lance was identified by some interpreters as
the lance on which the sponge of vinegar was offered to
the dying Christ. Such scriptural stories as that of
Lazarus, in which Christ is the healer of death, though
the dead man has the responsibility of faith if he is to
receive the healing, can be correlated thematically with
the medicine man healing the dead man in the pre-Chris-
tian nature rituals or the knight healing the Fisher King
in the post-Christian romances. Or to extend symbols,
Christ going through the trial of crucifixion in order to
save mankind from its death-in-life brings the total

Scriptures into the shape of the quest pattern. One must keep constantly in mind that Christ is one of the great spring gods. His physical birth is even now celebrated by an evergreen tree lit with candles, giving in the midst of winter promise of the light to come, and his more important spiritual ascension beyond physical death is celebrated each spring with eggs and May-baskets and rabbits about the time young girls, dressed in white, dance around the beribboned May pole.

In formal church ritual, in lore, and in art, Christ is surrounded by the familiar accoutrements of the central gods of the ancient nature cults. Water is repeated in water for immersion, water for walking on, water for bathing feet, water for sprinkling heads. Light surrounds Christ in the sunlike halo; he is "the Prince of Light" warring with "the Prince of Darkness." The fish, that prolific creature of the water which can be multiplied many times to feed the people and which on certain fast days is eaten instead of meat, becomes his symbol of life as it was already in countless religions. His is the natural way of life: simplicity in clothing and food and shelter, suspicion of the rich and kindness to the poor, abnegation of the self from physical luxuries. Love and fertility are implicit in his every association, love in word after word and fertility, despite his own chastity, through such figures as Mary of the immaculate birth, the universal symbol for motherhood in the Western culture, and Mary Magdalene, the promiscuous one who has transcended the promiscuity of the flesh to the promiscuity of faith. It is extremely interesting that in some early versions of the Bible Christ is referred to as the Orient, that is, the rising one, and maybe even then implicitly the one of the East, whence each morning

comes assurance that light follows darkness, rising follows
a fall. Variously, people face the east to worship, "go
west" to die, and are buried facing the east to be reborn.
The grail knights on their passage through the waste
land generally moved from west to east to quest the
grail and effect salvation.

The story of the quest for the grail and its multi-
cultural symbolic implications Eliot interweaves throughout his poem. He presents modern man in a futile search
for love and faith moving through the waste land of his
world. The definition of this modern man is an inclusive
one, for the voices through which the poet speaks are variously those of the aristocratic (mannered, functionless,
nostalgic for a dead past), the *nouveaux-riches* (gauche,
bored, amoral), the economically insecure (ugly, vulgar,
animalistic). The modern prototype goes through several steps of seeking. In part I, "The Burial of the Dead,"
he feels death in spring, expresses himself through the
decadent aristocracy, hears a fortuneteller misusing the
Tarot cards nevertheless reveal to him that he will not
find "the Hanged Man" and that he should fear "death
by water," instead of purification and rebirth. The
Hanged Man is a traditional scapegoat image and, as
Eliot points out, Christ reference. In part II, "A Game
of Chess," he learns the arbitrariness of life and speaks
sordidly of love-making through the bored rich and the
horribly physical poor. In part III, "The Fire Sermon,"
his ordeal by fire as it were, he sees in the Thames a
death rather than a flowing image. He reveals his quest,
this time as an Eastern merchant, as more commercial
than spiritual. He hears a universal Tiresias, who has
been both man and woman, describe the routine affairs
of clerks and stenographers and laments the passing of

the grand passions of the Renaissance and pre-Renaissance times. If the seeker wants to be freed of the "fire of lust," he seems hardly successful, for in this section fire seems to have been more destructive than purifying. In part IV, "Death by Water," the prediction of the fortuneteller of part I is fulfilled, for here the seeker, "Phlebas the Phoenician," is drowned rather than resurrected. It has been pointed out that etymologically *Phlebas* is both *phallos* as related to the "commerce of lust" and *vein* as used in "vein of commerce," suggesting the Phoenician as missionary for his Eastern fertility cult and as merchant. Eliot's modern Phoenician seems to serve only the latter materialistic function. Phlebas, we are told, "Forgot the cry of gulls." Twice earlier in the poem, nightingales, recalling the change of Philomel into a bird so that she could escape rape by a cruel king, have cried "jug jug," perhaps to remind us of the ever-present danger of the materialistic rape of the spirit in our times. In part V, "What the Thunder Said," the modern quester continues, alas, on a symbolic walk to Emmaus. The reference to the Biblical Emmaus bears out the prediction that the quester will not find "the Hanged Man," just as the disciples who have left Christ in the grave do not recognize him as the hooded figure beside them, do not, that is, heed the call to rebirth. He is already in and will remain in a waste land of "no water but only rock," "dry sterile thunder without rain," and "red sullen faces" sneering and snarling "From doors of mud-cracked houses." Even more significantly, the waste land is a land of the end of things: "Falling towers/ Jerusalem Athens Alexandria/ Vienna London." The Perilous Chapel is "empty"—the meaningful trials are not even there to endure. Instead of the passionate cry of the nightingale or the warning of the gulls above the water to man, on and finally in the water, he hears through the empty chapel only the cock's crow, a traditional song of betrayal. The thunder with its direction to "give," "sympathize," and "control" is heard at last, as if in a sudden gust of rain, but the question is whether it reaches the ears of the modern quester. The voice of the poem, usually that of the futile quester and hence more the promise of death than of salvation, becomes now the voice of the modern Fisher King, impotent, sterile, having failed in his responsibility to his people, resigned to continuation in his waste land. "Fishing, with the arid plains behind me," he asks, "Shall I at least set my lands in order?" He prays with the words of the thunder, adding the desire for "the Peace that passeth understanding." The reader is hardly left with hope that the prayer will be consummated.

Needless to say, books have been written on the sources, implications, and details of the grail legend and about as many words have been devoted to Eliot's use of it as an ironic objective correlative. I say *ironic* because Eliot's quester is doomed to failure in his eastward (sunward, godward, loveward) journey by his misplaced values, by the nature of the society itself, and by the dreadful emptiness of the chapel when he gets, at least physically, where he is going. In most of the poem Eliot's quester is in fact a commercial man of the East who has come to the waste land of the West. Marlow's quest, just as fraught with terrors as that of Eliot's prototype or, we have suggested, of Hemingway's Nick, ends assuringly in moral victory, in a belief in the potentialities of man. The more sophisticated adherents of naturalism in the 'twenties wanted to emphasize the futile end

of seeking, and even the practitioners of prose saw that
Eliot had worked out a highly effective method for
making the point.

Fitzgerald's *The Great Gatsby*, in many ways the
most representative novel of the 'twenties, combines
strikingly all of the elements about which we have been
talking: the central intelligence, the journey of learning for the focus of narration, the accomplished experience of a dramatically sensational central character who
serves as the central lesson, the structure of a mythic
quest ending in the irony of disappointment, the use then
of grail imagery in the ambivalent mock and serious
manner of Eliot, and evidence of a constant and specific
awareness of Eliot's *Waste Land.*

Fitzgerald's Nick Carraway is a carefully handled
narrator who, like Hemingway's central intelligence
Nick Adams, gives the entire organization to the story.
In a sense Gatsby is no more the dramatic center of
The Great Gatsby than are the killers or Ole Andreson
in "The Killers." Again, these characters, and we might
add Conrad's Kurtz here, are all accomplished examples
from which the innocent observer learns the way of the
world. If we can reconstruct Kurtz's or Gatsby's development, or even conjecture about Ole Andreson's
("He was in the ring, you know;" "I wonder what he
did?" "Double-crossed somebody. That's what they kill
them for."), we hardly see any one of them change
dramatically. The action involving change from exposition through complication to climax and denouement all
happens within or to the focus of narration. Marlow
learns, Nick learns, and now in Fitzgerald another Nick
learns; Kurtz, Ole, and Gatsby are the examples of whatever reality the innocent narrator must face.

It is hardly coincidence that Hemingway's Nick
Adams and Fitzgerald's Nick Carraway bear the same
first names. Fitzgerald's Nick, talking in the first person,
recalls his "more vulnerable years"—Hemingway's characters "wound" early and build up defenses later—when
his father taught him a sensitivity to the plight of others.
He has come from the West, where his family has been
"prominent" and "well-to-do" for generations. He has
been in the war and has come back "restless." Fitzgerald,
who was disappointed as a young officer stuck in New
York City and never got overseas into combat, passes
over the war experience with a flip remark, although
Hemingway, Dos Passos, and others more directly involved make the war the educating, wounding experience. Nick's is yet to come, but at first he responds to
his traditional home in the West as if he had been
through the works and is ready for expatriation. His
home suddenly seems "like the ragged edge of the universe," and with his family's blessing he sets out "in the
spring of twenty-two" to be a bondsalesman in the East,
"permanently, I thought." He has begun his quest,
which has at best a kind of mock materialistic goal.
Compare, say, the goal of Eliot's Phoenician merchant
on a modern commercial and lecherous quest rather than
on the traditional one for faith and love. In any case,
Nick is out in the world alone and extremely aware of
being so. His room in the city is hot and uncomfortable,
and since he "had just left a country of wide lawns and
friendly trees," he takes a house out on Long Island, com-
muting distance from his job. The house is not exactly a
reproduction of his age-old home in its more or less pastoral setting. It is small, somewhat run-down, overshad-
owed by the gauche mansion of Gatsby next door (as it

later turns out), and furthermore at West Egg rather than
East Egg, the more fashionable part of the island. There
is distinct irony here. He has left the West to begin his
life anew only to end up at West Egg, though Fitzgerald
makes the point that East Egg, like West Egg, is "crushed
flat at the contact end" to the island and that the two
places seem no different at all to "the gulls that fly overhead." Recall that in Eliot, Phlebas the Phoenician forgot
the cry of the warning gulls flying above him. Only the
"wingless" are impressed by the illusion of differences
which are learned and social instead of fundamental and
natural. Still, as soon as Nick is given some sense of belonging when a nameless quester "more recently arrived
than I" asks helplessly, "How do I get to West Egg village?" he feels that life has promise:

And so with the sunshine and the great bursts of leaves
growing on the trees, just as things grow in fast movies, I
had that familiar conviction that life was beginning over
again with the summer.

The inclusion of a modern, commercial image such as
"fast movies" of course inverts in tone what might have
had the assuring connotation of rebirth and growth. It is,
after all, a false spring since it is already an impressively
hot summer. Incidentally, Henry and Catherine in *A
Farewell to Arms* experience a false spring just before
death comes, and even worse, to Eliot's spokesman,
"April is the cruelest month, breeding / Lilacs out of the
dead land" because the speaker does not feel the regeneration that should come at this time. Nick vows to bring
back into his life the "literary" interests of his past college days, but the reader has doubt: he has already surrounded himself with books on banking and investment

which promise "to unfold the shining secrets that only
Midas and Morgan and Maecenas knew." The source of
the romance of the grail quest was in effect initiation
rites into mysteries invoking faith and love, perhaps suggested here in a kind of inverse imagery. With a certain
awe at the glittering "white palaces of fashionable East
Egg," Nick goes to the very place to have lunch with his
distant cousin Daisy and her husband Tom Buchanan.
Like Nick, they too have come from the West, but they
have all the appearance of East-Eggers, that is, for
"wingless" observers who pay attention to the right
clubs, the right colleges, well-appointed houses, cor-
rectly served meals, all that money obtained long enough
ago can eventually buy. One begins to suspect that there
are no true Easterners and no true East to be found.
Nick, in fact, feels uneasy in the Buchanan home. The
impressive thing about Tom is his "cruel body" and his
confidence that the "white race" should be kept "dominant." Daisy and her visitor Jordan Baker, both dressed
in white, give Nick the impression of impermanency, as
if they are floating around the room, though Daisy's
"bright" eyes and mouth and "exciting voice" convey
"a promise that she had done gay, exciting things just a
while since and that there were gay, exciting things hov-
ering in the next hour." Daisy and Jordan carry on chit-
chat with Nick in an aura of gold-and-white imagery. "I
always watch for the longest day of the year and then
miss it," says Daisy. "We ought to plan something,"
yawns Jordan. "What do people plan?" asks Daisy
"helplessly." "It was sharply different from the West,"
Nick says to the reader, and to Daisy he confesses, "You
make me feel uncivilized. . . . Can't you talk about crops
or something?" The air of promise about the absolutely

correct place is changed abruptly into "tense gayety" when Tom's mistress, Myrtle Wilson, calls and Daisy and Jordan talk openly about Tom's affair while they are eavesdropping on his telephone conversation. At last Nick is literally in East Egg, but his own quest has begun to pall: "To a certain temperament the situation might have seemed intriguing—my own instinct was to telephone immediately for the police." One recalls Nick Adams' "Don't you want to go and see the police?" when he, another innocent, comes face to face with evil and death. Tom and Jordan walk back into the library "as if to a vigil beside a perfectly tangible body"; Nick and Daisy walk into the "deep gloom" of the veranda. Daisy professes her cynicism, her sterile reluctance to have had a child, a desire for her child to be a "beautiful little fool," her "ennui," an ironic nostalgia for her "white girlhood" in St. Louis.

It made me uneasy [says Nick], as though the whole evening had been a trick of some sort to exact a contributary emotion from me. I waited, and sure enough, in a moment she looked at me with an absolute smirk on her lovely face, as if she had asserted her membership in a rather distinguished secret society to which she and Tom belonged.

Again, the "secret society" imagery suggests the mysteries into which the virginal youths of the grail quest were initiated. Jordan is revealed as *the* Jordan Baker, a much publicized golf champion, indeed one of the heroines of the culture. Nick contends that he is not engaged to a girl out West; in fact, he reveals to the reader that one reason he had come East was to avoid being "rumored into marriage." That he has come East in part to flee love adds further irony in juxtaposition to the

traditional quest. Nick leaves the Buchanan place, "con-
fused" and "a little disgusted," feeling that he should get
Daisy "to rush out of the house, child in arms"—a romantic if natural thought, like Nick Adams' suggestion that
Ole Andreson simply leave the spot of his destined death.
At home he sees on the lawn next door Gatsby, about
whom Jordan has already inquired: Gatsby is stretching
"out his arms toward the dark water in a curious way,"
"trembling," in the direction of a "small green light,"
which turns out to be at the end of the Buchanans' pier,
toward the very setting which has all but frightened
Nick.

Taken in itself, the story of Nick Carroway in
Chapter I which we have just reviewed is in effect the
story of Nick Adams in "The Killers." The innocent
comes face to face with evil and death, but in a much
more complicated social sense, and responds in highly
traditional ways—call the police, or get out of here. But
he is "disgusted," not yet hardened, simply on the way
to being so. The entire novel completes the pessimistic
learning cycle of Nick Carroway just as Hemingway's
total group of stories completes that of Nick Adams.

The closeness of Hemingway may be a predictable
similarity growing out of similar themes, but innumerable details indicate that Fitzgerald consciously borrowed
from *The Waste Land* to emphasize the futility of the
modern quest. The chapter which we have described is
followed by a description to which Fitzgerald returns
several times in the novel:

About half way between West Egg and New York the
motor road hastily joins the railroad and runs behind it for
a quarter of a mile, so as to shrink away from a certain
desolate area of land. This is a valley of ashes—a fantastic

farm where ashes grow like wheat into ridges and hills
and grotesque gardens; where ashes take the forms of houses
and chimneys and rising smoke and, finally, with a transcendent effort, of ash-gray men, who move dimly and already crumbling through the powdery air. Occasionally a
line of gray cars crawls through an invisible track, gives out
a ghastly creak, and comes to rest, and immediately the
ash-gray men swarm up with leaden spades and stir up an
impenetrable cloud, which screens their obscure operations
from your sight.

But above the gray land and the spasms of black dust
which drift endlessly over it, you perceive, after a moment
the eyes of Doctor T. J. Eckleburg. The eyes of Doctor T.
J. Eckleburg are blue and gigantic—their retinas are one
yard high. They look out of no face, but, instead, from
a pair of enormous yellow spectacles which pass over a non-
existent nose. Evidently some wild wag of an oculist set
them there to fatten his practise in the borough of Queens,
and then sank down himself into eternal blindness, or forgot them and moved away. But his eyes, dimmed a little by
many paintless days, under sun and rain, brood on over
the solemn dumping ground.

The valley of ashes is bounded on one side by a small
foul river, and, when the drawbridge is up to let barges
through, the passengers on waiting trains can stare at the
dismal scene for as long as half an hour. There is always
a halt of at least a minute. . . .

Not only do we have here the more symbolic than realistic waste land through which men pass every day from
the city to the Eggs (flattened ones, we have been told),
but a blind and neglected Fate or God-figure in Doctor
T. J. Eckleburg. One thinks of the medicine man in the
nature rituals who makes the dead come alive and of
Christ as "the Healer," but one can hardly expect any in-
terference from this faceless, noseless doctor. In fact, it

is near this waste land, under the very eyes of Eckleburg, that Daisy and Tom directly and Gatsby, Nick, and Jordan indirectly bring death to Tom's mistress, Myrtle Wilson, and subsequently to Gatsby himself and to Wilson. Following the scene of Myrtle's death, her husband George Wilson is questioned by his neighbor, the young Greek restaurant owner Michaelis. "Ever had any children? . . . Have you got a church you go to sometime, George? . . . Maybe I could call up the church and get a priest to come over and he could talk to you, see? . . . Didn't you get married in a church? . . . Maybe you got some friend that I could telephone for, George?" The answers are all negative to the very questions of fertility, faith, and love that Eliot is concerned with in his *Waste Land*. Wilson only turns his eyes "out to the ash heaps" and repeats his accusation of Myrtle: "God knows what you've been doing. You may fool me, but you can't fool God!" The bewildered Michaelis is shocked to see that Wilson "is looking at the eyes of Doctor T. J. Eckleburg, which had just emerged, pale and enormous, from the dissolving night." "God sees everything," Wilson insists. "That's an advertisement," answers Michaelis, no longer able to look at the false, indifferent God.

That Michaelis, who shows a serious sensitivity to man's need for faith and love and recognizes furthermore the lack of faith in an advertising, commercial world, is a youthful *Greek* restaurant owner may be the chance use of character stereotypes to which Fitzgerald is disposed in the case of minor characters. Or it may be that Fitzgerald puts the words of a sincere demand for belief and love in the mouth of a character who is young but old-world, even implicitly classical in background, just as Eliot constantly contrasts the meagerness of con-

temporary feelings to the grand passions of Elizabethan
and classical times. Fitzgerald's readiness to employ
stereotypes is seen again in the names of T. J. Eckleburg,
the tin god, and Wolfsheim, the gangster with whom
Gatsby has been associated. Wolfsheim, Fitzgerald repeatedly states, is a Jew. The intention perhaps is to remind the reader that Gatsby, seeking the East in the
fashionable Daisy, is associated with a man who is alien
to the sought-for society, who simply doesn't or isn't allowed to belong. Wolfsheim's lack of honest involvement in the culture is further dramatized by his reputedly having fixed a World Series. If Michaelis with
his old-world faith and warmth is shocked by Wilson's
even unknowingly putting his faith in an advertisement,
Nick as the innocent is no less shocked by finding dis-
honesty in the epitome of American sports.

A similar shock in Nick's learning is of course his
discovery that Jordan Baker, a nationally known golf-
champion, is dishonest in her game and, what is more important, dishonest in her personal relationships. She hates
"careless people" because they might not get out of the
way of her own carelessness: that, she says, is why she
likes the innocent Nick. Nick in reply says of himself
quite early in the book: "I am one of the few honest
people that I have ever known"—all of which brings us
back to the point that the journey of learning around
which the book is structured is Nick's, not Gatsby's, and
certainly not anybody else's.

Gatsby is pursuing a dream, yes ("romantic readiness"), but it is a self-deluding, false dream ("everything
for which I have an unaffected scorn"). If he invents even
a fabulous Eastern past for himself, if he wants to become one with Daisy who is East for him, if he thinks

that the East is all silk shirts and big parties and "old sports," his values are already misplaced, or in terms of the quest itself, his quest from the beginning is conspicuously futile. And even *he* should know this, as Tom so carefully points out, for after all, behind the character he has made himself into, are Wolfsheim and under-the-counter liquor and half-truths. "There are only the pursued, the pursuing, the busy and the tired," Nick says at one stage of his learning. Gatsby is probably one of "the pursuing," but again we see him only as an accomplished character whose background, much like Kurtz's, is filled in with innumerable hindsights and bits of rumor. He does not develop within the scope of the story, and he really learns nothing. Nick may see that Gatsby's coming face to face with his dream has destroyed it, he may learn that the past can't be repeated, he too may feel that Gatsby is demanding too much of Daisy when he wants her never to have loved even Tom. But Gatsby dies waiting for word from Daisy even when the most naïve person would have seen that he was trapped by the careless Buchanans. Gatsby is a quester in Nick's eyes: in his "silver suit," committed "to the following of a grail," keeping his "sacred vigil" outside of Daisy's house, once feeling when he left her house that "if he had searched harder, he might have found her—that *he* was leaving her behind" (my italics). But it is left for Nick both to admire the "pursuers" even in a futile quest ("They're a rotten crowd. . . . You're worth the whole damn bunch put together") and, alas, to know that when Daisy "vanished into her rich house, into her rich, full life," she left Gatsby "—Nothing."

Nick's learning that the East he sought as well as that pursued by Gatsby is after all a waste land need not be traced step by step from the rich house where he feels the police should be called, to the sordid apartment of Myrtle and Tom where an actual brawl occurs, to the gauche parties at Gatsby's where even the moon seems prepared by a caterer. He moves back and forth between these settings learning new disappointments, new despairs. Actually the very group whom Eliot employs in *The Waste Land* to reveal the contemporary nothingness is similarly composed of the aristocrats, the *nouveaux riches,* and the vulgar, and it is not inconceivable that Fitzgerald saw the analogy here. Once when Nick and Gatsby have just passed by the "valley of ashes" which connects Fitzgerald's scenes as it does Eliot's, Nick hears the familiar "jug-jug-spat!" of the motorcycle of a policeman out to arrest Gatsby for speeding. "Jug-jug-spat!" is hardly a common sound for a motorcycle, but a recognizable one for the reader who recalls the "jug jug" of Eliot's nightingales warning against the rape of the world. Other details just as specifically parody and suggest Eliot and add up to emphasizing that Fitzgerald, with Eliot in mind, was writing a prose *Waste Land.* His modern quester, Nick, seeks in vain love, faith, the romantic, the exotic, a beginning, all of the values with which East, as the source of the sun, is traditionally associated. He reaches the age of thirty, "the promise of a decade of loneliness, a thinning list of single men to know, a thinning brief-case of enthusiasm, [and Prufrock-like] thinning hair," and with all of these no girl. He literally drives "on toward Death." Gatsby, from whom ironically he learns the falseness of the East on its literal and symbolic level, dies in a mixture of dream and ash imagery. "Blessed are the dead the rain falls on," says someone in as highly an ironic context as Eliot's initial reference to April of which *his* quester also doesn't partake. "Amen," says the owl-eyed man, a kind of walking Eckleburg, and he adds the epitaph of pathos: "The poor son-of-a-bitch."

Nick returns West, declaring himself, Gatsby, Jordan, Tom, and Daisy, all born Westerners, as "subtly unadaptable to Eastern life," and recalling the East, or "West Egg especially," in a pantomime of death, directionlessness, materialism, indifference, and coldness.

Even when the East excited me most, even when I was most keenly aware of its superiority to the bored, sprawling, swollen towns beyond the Ohio, with their iterminable inquisitions which spared only the children and the very old—even then it had always for me a quality of distortion. West Egg, especially, still figures in my more fantastic dreams. I see it as a night scene by El Greco: a hundred houses, at once conventional and grotesque, crouching under a sullen, overhanging sky and a lustreless moon. In the foreground four solemn men in dress suits are walking along the sidewalk with a stretcher on which lies a drunken woman in a white evening dress. Her hand, which dangles over the side, sparkles cold with jewels. Gravely the men turn in at a house. But no one knows the woman's name, and no one cares.

All left at the end is Gatsby's empty house with an obscene word on the steps, just as Eliot's quester finds even the Perilous Chapel empty: trialless and grailless.

It is clear that *The Waste Land* was both a conscious and an unconscious correlative for Fitzgerald. As in the case of Hemingway, Fitzgerald may have been made aware by Eliot of the pattern and meaning of the grail quest and its sources in vegetation and initiation rites. Whether he got his quest imagery first or second-hand, whether he used it consciously or unconsciously, he *did* employ it to make his mock point of the absence of love, of faith, and of the capacity for regeneration in our time. To be sure, Nick moves from the West to the East for traditional, meticulous reasons, but Fitzgerald mocks the commercial and social purposes of modern man by juxtaposing a framework of modern, materialistic references and the language of universal hope and rebirth: eggs and leaves bursting out on trees and promise and shining gold and chaste white. It is hardly by chance that Fitzgerald's physical East has the illusory surface of a spiritual East associated with the various worships of the sun gods. Nick wanting to be a successful bondsalesman and Gatsby wanting to enter the secret society of Daisy are not far afield in many senses of the word from Eliot's making the modern quester a merchant.

Eliot, of course, is painfully intellectual in a way that Hemingway and Fitzgerald are not—or it may be the difference between a modern esoteric poetry and a modern prose which can be read both as literal narrative and as symbolic creed. The Hanged Man, the universal image for the scapegoat necessary for purification, is missing from Eliot's Tarot deck, and Eliot makes the most of Christ unrecognized, of spring not felt, of movement west instead of east. He sees and utilizes fully the similar patterns from cultural framework to cultural framework. He brings the lack of Christ in, but only as one meaning out of many.

To a less rich extent, but perhaps in a more satisfactory one for narrative prose, Fitzgerald makes the failure of his East more than the failure of a place or even of a way of life. There are ultimately in *The Great Gatsby* no well-mannered, rich East, no true Easterners,

no Eastern values that demand respect on any level. Like
Gatsby, we are left in our silver armor with no illusions
about the secret societies of the East, keeping our lonely
vigil over Nothing. It is not far from this statement to a
statement of no spiritual East, no Orient, no Rise after a
Fall, no archetypal Christ as medicine man, healer, savior, regenerator, warmth-giving sun-god. If Fitzgerald,
employing the traditional grail imagery, does not make
the next step to associated Christ imagery as did Eliot,
the point is implicitly, as in much fiction of the 'twenties,
that faith is lacking and the pursued ideals are illusory.

The journey of the discovery of nothingness is a
familiar structure in post-World War I literature in
contrast to Conrad's journey of the discovery of the innate moral sense of man or of his tragic potentialities.
Conrad criticized the naturalists implicitly by employing
in, say, *Lord Jim*, Christian imagery to point up his
meaning. The writers influenced by naturalistic monism
and determinism learned from Eliot to mock the quest
for values by employing its very imagery, Christian or
otherwise, in a highly ironic context.

BIBLIOGRAPHICAL NOTE:

JOURNEY, QUEST, AND CORRELATIVE

Cleanth Brooks and Robert Penn Warren in *Understanding Fiction* (New York, 1943), a text which has influenced the critical reading habits of an entire generation, present a rich interpretation of "The Killers" which has directly influenced my own interpretation. An excellent approach to Hemingway, one full of suggestions not always developed, is Philip Young's *Hemingway* (New York, 1952). There are as many guides to the allusiveness of Eliot's *The Waste Land* and as many paraphrases and summaries imposing an easy continuity upon it as there are guides and restatements of Joyce's *Ulysses* and, now, *Finnegan's Wake*. Particularly useful guides are George Williamson's *A Reader's Guide to T. S. Eliot* (New York, 1953) and such meticulous explications as those in Brooks and Warren's *Understanding Poetry* (New York, 1950) and in Kimon Friar and John Malcolm Brinnin's *Modern Poetry* (New York, 1951). I pay respect to Jessie Weston's *From Ritual to Romance* (Cambridge, 1920) because it *was* in Eliot's awareness and hence in the awareness of Fitzgerald, Hemingway, Faulkner, and others, knowing full well that among anthropologists and medievalists Miss Weston's book is now considered naïve, too simple, or actually wrong. But like Freud or Marx or Frazer, she must be considered a pioneer in a way of thinking that has been modified, refined, and paradoxically denied by its very extenders.

Christ As Social Scapegoat:

FAULKNER'S
Light in August

FOR the writers of
the twentieth-century "temper," Conrad's conscious creation of tragedy and his serious employment of the Christ
pattern to make his point were intellectually out of
date. If at all, the religious frame of reference func-
tioned in the important novels from 1900 to 1930 nega-
tively to produce irony and pathos. The poetry of T. S.
Eliot, so rich in the mock analogies between the hopeless
plight of modern man and the faith of Lazarus, the gran-
deur of Dante, the magnanimity of Hamlet, and indeed
the intensity of Kurtz, gave to the writers of prose a
technique for emphasizing the purposelessness and in-
fidelity of contemporary life. Faulkner, interestingly
enough in the light of his more recent *A Fable,* was one
of the most fruitful employers of the Eliotesque method
of the ironic analogy, and his most frequent analogy,
even at the beginning, was to the legend of Christ. Like
Fitzgerald, Faulkner was consciously aware of Eliot as a
frame of reference. In *Pylon* (1935), which has to do
with those initiated into the cult of the machine, he even

named one chapter "The Love Song of Prufrock," suggesting among other things the ineffectualness of the
men who, full of the sense of responsibility, guilt, remorse, are not free to act because they do not realize
their freedom.

In the novels which appeared at the end of the
'twenties, one almost senses the Eliot of *The Waste Land*
—or at least that Faulkner's correlatives were the same as
Eliot's. *Soldier's Pay* (1926) has for its center a kind of
golden boy who, after his experience in World War I, is
wandering lost in America in a state of catatonic shock,
as near a living death as a man alive can be. The attempts
to resurrect him through the attentions of several men and
women, representing a variety of kinds of devotion, fail,
and he is freed, if at all, in death. One is reminded on the
one hand of Faulkner's subadar in the short story "Ad
Astra" who insists that "all this generation which fought
in the war are dead," though they "do not know it yet,"
and on the other hand of Eliot's use of the Fisher King,
mysteriously wounded in the genitals, waiting in vain for
an agent of purity and vitality to resuscitate him for the
reclaiming of his barren land. A member of the dead
generation figuring in "Ad Astra" is Bayard Sartoris,
who appears in 1929 as the protagonist of the novel *Sartoris*. Bayard is searching for rebirth after he has lived
with death in the war: his twin John, his more artistic,
gentler half, has been killed, in part through Bayard's
failure of responsibility for his life. In his quest, Bayard
goes through a series of ritualistic steps whereby, almost
like the mutilated Fisher King, he tries to reinvigorate
himself. Everything fails—the old values of the feudal
system, the new religion of speed; brotherhood through
the throwing over of the traditional class differences, ro-

mantic courtship; proof of physical virility, the pastoral escape; etc. That Bayard is really seeking a spiritual re-birth from the symbolic waste land in which he exists is pointed up forcefully by Faulkner's use of Christ-imagery in the last part of the novel. Bayard, wandering, arrives at a Negro cabin on Christmas Eve. He is allowed to sleep in a manger-like shed, but he passes a fitful, cold night—in a passage characterized by death-images instead of the life-images he is seeking. The next day, Christmas, he enters the Negro house where the couple and their three children share their meager Christmas with Bayard. Their celebration is in sharp contrast to the abundant one which is being celebrated at the Sartoris plantation house, but without this abundance the Negroes' Christmas is a sincere and thankful one. At the climax of the scene Bayard drinks with the Negroes in what could conceivably be a true communion, considering the dis-crimination of the Southern system of which Faulkner makes so much in this book and in others. In some way, this scene suggests what Bayard has been seeking: love, simplicity, faith in spite of hardship; but he is neverthe-less out of it, realistically speaking, and unprepared for it, dramatically speaking. He continues on his journey, moving farther away from his family, including his preg-nant wife. Finally, he arrives at a railroad station where shines, instead of an "evening star," an electric light bulb. The story is in effect over: Bayard wanders summarily to his death in an airplane, isolated even from the birth of the son who will continue him. In a sense, Bayard is both the wise man seeking Christ and Christ seeking transcendence. He is on a kind of futile "Journey of the Magi," and he is also struggling for a Christ-like rebirth from his death-in-life, but in vain.

Perhaps the most interesting example of Faulkner's use of the Christ frame of reference is *Light in August* (1932). It is an amusing book and it is a moving book. But it is also an embarrassing book, for it contains so many guide posts to the author's central intention that the reader feels he is looking in on an author creating nakedly with the shades up. Still, I hasten to add that the book does not force its analogies in the way that the later *A Fable* does. The suggestions of related meanings are admittedly strong and clear, but the drama at hand stands up on its own and simply attains richness and depth through the implied correlatives. That Faulkner gives the reader clear-cut directions to more basic meanings, primarily through names or puns on names, may have been originally a kind of joke, which was even funnier to the author in that so many critics missed it. Early in the book he has a character Byron Bunch remember "that he had even thought how a man's name, which is supposed to be just the sound for who he is, can be somehow an augur of what he will do, if other men can only read the meaning in time." Faulkner says in effect: understand the names which I employ, and you will not only understand but indeed predict the pattern of behavior of the characters throughout the novel.

The first important character whom we meet is Lena Grove, innocently pregnant by her not so innocent lover Lucas Burch. Having learned that she is with child, the irresponsible, amoral Lucas has left with a false promise to send for Lena when he gets a job. When her pregnancy begins to be apparent, Lena leaves the home of the lumber-worker brother with whom she lives, to search naïvely for Lucas. The brother has worked at a mill which has been through seven years of productivity cut-

ting pines and "in seven years more . . . would destroy
all the timber within its reach." The brother calls Lena a
whore: he has, Faulkner tells us, lost the softness and
tenderness of his youth in his hard work and replaced it
only with "a kind of stubborn and despairing fortitude
and the bleak heritage of his blood-pride." Lena sets out
"with her swelling and unmistakable burden," repeated
in "a small cloth bundle" which she holds. She is wearing
"a shapeless garment of faded blue" and carrying "a
palm-leaf fan." In a way completely naïve and amusing
she passes for four weeks along "a peaceful corridor
paved with unflagging and tranquil faith and peopled
with kind and nameless faces and voices . . . backrolling
now behind her a long monotonous succession of peaceful and undeviating changes from day to dark and dark
to day again, through which she advanced in identical
and anonymous and deliberate wagons as though through
a succession of creak-wheeled and limpeared avatars,
like something moving forever and without progress
across an urn."

In the very few pages from which these quotations
come, Faulkner has almost appealed for recognition of the
function of Lena Grove in the novel as a whole. Certainly she suggests Mary in her blue garb, though it has
markedly faded since the conventional azure with which
the Renaissance painters clothed the Virgin. Her relation
with Lucas has been on her part innocent and loving
rather than promiscuous, though unloving people like
her brother are incapable of understanding this. The actual father of the child has disappeared, and eventually
Byron Bunch will become her protector by proxy and
finally her husband. Predictably too she and Byron will
have difficulty finding a place in which the child may be

born. The palm-fan which she carries is a distinctly
Southern accoutrement, but in the context of the striking
Mary analogy one recalls the palms of Palm Sunday that
usher Christ into Jerusalem at the beginning of the holy
week. Sir James Frazer points to several uses of the palm
in fertility rituals to produce rain or to make the seeds
grow, which recall of course the function of Mary as a
goddess of love, though an immaculate one, and as a goddess of fertility, though a chaste one. Still, it is the name
of Lena Grove that is her chief revelation. One need go
no farther than any Webster's unabridged dictionary to
discover that Lena is "the diminutive of Magdalene and
Helen," two names which conveniently bridge the
Christian and Greek symbols for love and femaleness.
But Lena in her Mary imagery and in her complete
naïvete, though with child, is the pure one, somehow
more Diana-like than Helen-like. But as Frazer again reminds us, Diana was originally a great fertility goddess
whose rites were celebrated usually in a sacred *grove*
where she shared honors with a loved one, a male part-
ner, the predecessors of the priests known as Kings of
the Wood. Diana, incidentally, was usually represented
by an outstanding tree, in several recorded instances by
the beech tree.

Lena Grove, then, is apparently a goddess of love
and fertility, moving indeed through Faulkner's South
(as Faulkner has the boy's father say in "The Bear": he
has to talk about something) though she is the fertility
goddess of every culture: Oriental ("a succession of avatars"), Classical (Helen, Diana), Christian (Mary, Magdalene), and anything else you can think of in the past
and yet to come ("identical and anonymous . . . moving
forever"). Understand her name, and you know that she

will move through the drylands, reviving those who are dead in the many ways that the word can suggest. The men help her in her journey for reasons that they can't define; the women, like the significantly named hard-working Martha, feed her even when they don't want to. The place where she finally has her child is a servant's shack in the backyard of the old Burden plantation house, and in so doing she gives birth to life in a formerly dead setting. Miss Burden's defunct plantation home is the abode of death in a variety of ways. It is literal evidence of the *end* of a culture, the old South. It is the scene of the perversion of a religion, Calvinism, which Faulkner treats as a kind of Christianity without love and hence no Christianity at all. It is the reminder of the unloving concept of original sin; the South's *curse* in much of Faulkner is its making the Negro into a scape-goat, and Miss Burden here makes the South's discrimination her self-conscious *burden*. It is associated with the end of a female's productivity: Miss Burden reaches the time of menopause and literal death in the book's structure almost as Lena gives birth to her child. And it is the actual home of the lost-Christ, Faulkner's other main character, ironically named Christmas. The birth which Lena gives in the manifold-dead setting brings a final bit of love to the pathetic Mrs. Hines, dignity and freedom in death to the formerly Antichrist Christmas, and purpose to the self-consciously failed Reverend Gail Hightower. Finally, Lena moves farther north, as any spring goddess must do when the season demands it, ac-companied by the humorously named Byron Bunch (compare the closeness of Burch, who is not Beech, and of Bunch, who is not Burch, but certainly a richly am-biguous name on its own). Byron, previously so shy and even, Faulkner hints, in his relationship with Hightower previously homosexual, persists in his devotion to Lena. She accepts him calmly as her lover, as in effect the wood god to accompany her on her constant travels.

The very name of Lucas Burch is the transition between the story of Lena and the story of Joe Christmas, who is after all the conspicuous center of Faulkner's book. To Lena, the chaste and fertile one, he is the necessary tree god, though again he is Burch not Beech and hides even this slant-identification under the ordinary and springless name of Brown. As Byron Bunch later tells him, he has thrown away "twice inside of nine months what I ain't had in thirty-five years," that is, love of Lena and of the child which she bears by him. His relationship to Christmas is designated specifically as that of a "disciple" to a "master" with a name obviously derived from Luke who tells the story of Christ and from Judas who betrays his master to the deputies. By Byron's specific accusation of the betrayal of Lena, Lucas is doubly a Judas to the actual evidences of love as well as to the mock-evidences that may exist in Christmas. Ironically, he doesn't collect his thirty pieces for the capture of Christmas, who eludes him literally and symbolically. Lucas bows out of the novel by way of a freight train: he is a wanderer of course as Lena is and must leave when she gives birth to the child which resuscitates in one way or another practically every character in the book. That is, he must leave if he is to remain the personification of the denial of love incapable of a change in heart; penance is beside the point, for it is a concept attacked by Faulkner in this novel. Lucas' departure is preceded by a fight in which Byron Bunch, though beaten physically and in tone comically, proves himself the new champion, the serious substitute-father. To be sure, Byron is not named Joseph, yet he is after all more than Joseph since Lena is named Helen and Magdalene and not Mary. Rather as the lone one, the intense preacher, the constant searcher for love wherever he may find it, ultimately the romantic devotee to Lena's goddess of love, he is like the more famous Byron who preceded him.

That Lucas is a Judas is hardly his own moral failure, for the Christmas to whom he is a disciple is ostensibly an Antichrist, except for the beginning and end of his life. Space and time do not allow a complete tracing of Christmas' story, but as Faulkner says, the key is in the name if the readers will only use it. He is the son of the innocent Milly Hines and a wandering outsider. Compare of course Lena and Lucas, and note too that Milly's mother later tends Lena as if she were her own daughter. He is found on Christmas at the orphanage which names him, though he has obviously been born before Christmas, not exactly on that date. He is harrassed by a series of characters in the very name of Christianity. Old Hines, convinced that Christmas is his daughter's child by an itinerant Negro circus man, preaches in a Negro church a religion of hate and discrimination and punishment for sin. McEachern's religion would teach Christmas "to fear God and abhor idleness and vanity" with the typical Puritan's denial of love and understanding. Percy Grimm, who becomes the deputy to Christmas' final crucifixion, has a fascistic "faith in physical courage and blind obedience, and a belief that the white race is superior to all other races and that the American is superior to all other white races and that the American uniform is superior to all men." Like

Grimm, innumerable Southerners in the novel are violently pious with the mission of maintaining the God-ordained distinctions between persons. Even the little children are easily dissuaded from coming to him as children, and later the Negroes, the group with whom he has been identified by others and with whom he relentlessly identifies himself as Christ did with man, drive him from the church in which he cries out against the traditional God. All of the women who want to help him are deterred by the men who confuse absolute morality, diligence, thrift, law-and-order somehow with religion: his grandmother Mrs. Hines, the woman in charge of the orphanage, Mrs. McEachern, the waitress-prostitute Bobbie and the wife of the restaurant owner, even Miss Burden, whose social endeavor on behalf of Negroes is tied up with her Calvinist background and the very self-consciousness of her duty implicit in her name.

"You will find food and shelter and the care of Christian people," says Mr. McEachern when he takes him, adding on the same page, "Christmas. A heathenish name. Sacrilege. I will change that." Food is a unifying image throughout the book. Lena, whose welfare "the Lord will see to," is always fed when the need for food comes—at Martha's she had "a cup of coffee and a piece of cornbread," and with Martha's egg-money she buys cheese, crackers, and "a box of sardines," not only food, but such ritualistically proper food as bread and fish! But Christmas is tortured by the dietician whose official function is to sustain children but whose equation of love with sin feeds them only with hate. His early experiences of unnatural rejection make him expect the negation of emotion and suspect the pathetic reachings-out of women to nourish him. He destroys the food of Mrs. McEachern, he insists on paying Bobbie for the pie in the restaurant, he is ambivalent toward the suppers prepared by Miss Burden, accepting or rejecting them depending on the season of their affair. The innumerable references to the denial of food suggest the refusals of communion in its literal which *is* its symbolic sense or the unconsummated approach to meaningful love, in contrast of course to Christ's recurrent sincere communions and to Lena's unquestioned ones.

At the end of the novel, when Christmas is hunted *and* hungry, a Martha-like woman, frightened by his haggard appearance, refuses him help. He is forced to eat "rotting and wormriddled fruit," but he also gnaws "ripened ears of corn." Recalling the rejected food of Miss Burden, he experiences "a kind of writhing and excruciating agony of regret and remorse and rage." He becomes obsessed "not with food . . . but with the necessity to eat"; he eats "enormous quantities . . . with resultant crises of bleeding flux." He recalls even the Negroes feeding him in flight, but feeding him fearfully. "Of their brother afraid," he thinks in a tone so different from that with which he has insisted earlier on identification with Negroes in order to suffer with them, almost in order to arouse the hate of man rather than to transcend men's pathetic forgetting of love. The need for food becomes totally mystical as Christmas walks, comalike, with hardly awareness of touching the ground on a "dewgray" dawn. He shaves himself, preparing Christlike for his crucifixion—"It's Friday," a Negro tells Christmas, by this time "fleshless," timeless, placeless, "O Lawd God, it's Friday." He goes with an inspiring sense of purpose to face his death, some thirty years after his birth, and incidentally on the very day when Lena's child is born, to juxtapose death, sacrifice, crucifixion, resurrection, birth, the transcendence of food-as-the-body alone.

The important function of Miss Burden in her relationship with Christmas has already been mentioned briefly. In his twelfth chapter, Faulkner traces the phases of their affair:

During the first phase it had been as though he were outside a house where snow was on the ground, trying to get into the house; during the second phase he was at the bottom of a pit in the hot wild darkness; now he was in the middle of a plain where there was no house, not even snow, not even wind.

The spring of the affair is missing. The chapter begins with the second phase: "as though he had fallen into a sewer" which "ran only by night." The summer of the affair is described as "the wild throes of nymphomania" for Miss Burden as "a Beardsley of the time of Petronius might have drawn" and as a kind of "curiosity, pessimism . . . sheer inertia" for Christmas. This phase ends with Miss Burden's fatness, which is apparently obesity and not pregnancy. The ironic honeymoon of the summer which had no precedent spring ebbs into the autumnal meetings in the bedroom "as though they were married," with the insidious reminder of her Calvinist conscience and his sneaking off to Memphis whorehouses. This ends with her confusion of the cessation of flow accompanying the menopause and the cessation of flow accompanying pregnancy. The fourth phase, the very waste land of no house or snow or wind, is characterized by her desire "to make of him something between a hermit and a missionary to Negroes" by sending him to one of the colleges she supports. When she begins to pray for him with the Puritan's demands for "expiation" and "hell" and he refuses to join in her prayers, she prepares to shoot him, and he compulsively cuts her throat with the stereotype Negro's razor. Several emphases should be clarified here. She is the descendant of New Englanders, frontiersmen, Calvinists, whose religion of self-denial has kept her an unnatural spinster: her repressed emotions finally come out in physical expression in itself zealous, perverted, too late to be naturally productive. She is the descendant of the usurpers of the land and the especial betrayer of the earth which she has allowed to lie fallow. If the Southerners who built the decaying plantation house have destroyed themselves through their flaw of no-love in the curse of discrimination, her self-conscious morality as a woman carrying out her Christian duty has come no nearer to the natural love and fertility for which Faulkner seems to be making an effusive if elusive plea. Christmas with his razor makes her blood flow (and Burch sets fire to her house), which is destructive on one level of the final threat of the Calvinistic restraint of natural things and purifying on the other level in that it rids Christmas of the danger of giving in to this perversion of religion. It is as if in sacrificing her and the symbolic house in which she lives, Faulkner has cleansed Christmas to take on at last the function of scapegoat that he has refused but been attracted to throughout the book.

From the beginning of his life, Christmas had the role of social scapegoat imposed upon him by Mr. Hines, the children at the orphanage, the dietician, who considered him a "nigger" by that intangible and mystical set of Southern standards. One revenge for the hurt that he had suffered was ironically to insist on identification as a Negro to those who had taken him in as a white man. So long as he acted from motives of hate, Christmas appears as an Antichrist perverting and misusing his scapegoat function in a peculiarly self-pious way. The death of Miss Burden leads Christmas to accept and to play out the role for which he is destined. Recall our earlier discussion of Conrad's *black* and *white* puns in *Lord Jim* and *Heart of Darkness*. Faulkner's pervading pun is *Negro* and *white*. As a Southern writer, he makes the ironic point that man will transcend his plight in the world only when he ceases to resist the Negro in him, that is, when he admits his capacity for love, humility, and sacrifice. The Negro in Christmas and in any man is his capacity to endure the hurt for which man is destined in the world, in effect his capacity to be a Man. Man is born to die meaningfully. The archetypal woman, as dramatized in Lena, is born to endure beyond man's death, to live after the Negro she has borne has fulfilled his destiny, even so to give a continuity to life by bearing other Negroes to fulfill their destinies.

Left on the land is Lena to give birth to her child and to let Mrs. Hines triumph in attending the birth of the new Christmas, to make a man out of Byron, to give Hightower "purpose" after twenty-five years of doing nothing. Hightower, the minister who was too involved in the heroic past of his grandfather and his horses, always a male symbol in Faulkner and in mythology generally, to love his wife or to tend his congregation, administers to Lena at the birth of her child. He says of Miss Burden: "Poor barren woman. To have not lived only a week longer, until luck returned to this place. Until luck and life returned to these barren and ruined acres"—bringing together the social theme of the decayed South, the religious theme of resurrection out of a death which includes various religious distortions and especially Miss Burden's Calvinism, and the mythic theme of spring after winter, fertility after barrenness.

Hightower gives himself further courage and sacrifice when he claims that Christmas spent the night with him when he was supposed to have murdered Miss Burden. "Jesus Christ!" Grimm says, profanely pushing Hightower aside as he goes on to shoot Christmas and to emasculate him, according to the custom of lynchers punishing the dark rapers of white women. Emasculated at the very moment perhaps that Lena is suckling the new Christmas, the old Christmas "just lay there, with his eyes open and empty of everything save consciousness, and with something, a shadow, about his mouth." Faulkner surrounds his literal end with the simultaneous images of death and resurrection that suggest not Christ alone but all of the spring scapegoats of many religions:

For a long moment he looked up at them with peaceful and unfathomable and unbearable eyes. Then his face, body, all seemed to collapse, to fall in upon itself, and from out the slashed garments about his hips and loins the pent black blood seemed to rush like a released breath. It seemed to rush out of his pale body like the rush of sparks from a rising rocket; upon that black blast the man seemed to rise soaring into their memories forever and ever. They are not to lose it, in whatever peaceful valleys, beside whatever placid and reassuring streams of old age, in the mirroring faces of whatever children they will contemplate old disasters and newer hopes. It will be there, musing, quiet, steadfast, not fading and not particularly threatful, but of itself alone serene, of itself alone triumphant.

There is a question of course as to what has been the rejuvenating factor, the fertility goddess Lena or the newly evolved Christ-Dionysus figure Christmas. Christmas flows obviously like Christ on the cross and implicitly like Dionysus torn to pieces only to be made whole with each recurring spring. The serious sacrifice having been made by Christmas, Lena travels in a delightfully comic section with Byron and "her chap" presumably into some other region of the country farther north where "luck and life" have not yet returned.

One could go on forever recounting details that contribute to the patterns of Lena as a moving spring goddess of love and fertility and Christmas as a Christlike deity caught in the winter of personal and social hate and freed from it by the love and sacrifice which allow him his scapegoat function. The varieties of Christianity which emphasize anything except love are criticized severally. Conversely, references to the innumerable religions which celebrate the wonder of spring after winter are interwoven through the names of characters, the recurrence of universal rituals such as eating-the-god, and an imagery of endless roads which a succession of "avatars" traverse.

Coldly speaking, one finds in *Light in August* and in almost all of the novels of Faulkner an impressive anthropological approach far away from, though not exclusive of, the specific implications of a Southern social problem. The main result of his cultural relativity is a richness within the texture of the book which can never be recaptured through explication, but he keeps inviting analysis with explicit statements in the fiction itself. Still, the critic is embarrassed to say what he must say, even if simply to himself as a reader: "Look, here within the luxuriousness of characters and actions and emotions is a hint of the main continuity of meaning that

Faulkner is demanding." Stating the continuity may re-
duce the book to thin-sounding triteness, but criticism
is merely an abstraction from the whole and it must be
kept constantly in mind that the whole *is* there.

BIBLIOGRAPHICAL NOTE:

THE HERITAGE OF WESTERN CULTURE

The chief sources for an explication of this sort are simply
what one knows: a bit of Greek mythology, a bit of the Bible, a bit
of Oriental religion, some more of Faulkner. There have been many
explications of *Light in August,* most of them published since I first
presented the essence of this lecture informally at a University of
Michigan seminar in 1957, some of them overlapping my interpretation but never altogether so. *Modern Fiction Studies* has printed
three comments on *Light in August* and Faulkner, all of which have
some pertinence to my own: Beekman W. Cottrell, "Christian Symbols in *Light in August*" (Winter, 1956-1957), William H. F. Lamont,
"The Chronology of 'Light in August'" (Winter, 1957-1958), and
Donald Tritschler, "The Unity of Faulkner's Shaping Vision" (Winter, 1959-1960). The most provocative help in reading *Light in August,* however, is not other discussions of the book, including this
one, but the first section of Frazer's *The Golden Bough:* "The King
of the Wood." Frazer roams like Faulkner, but also like Faulkner,
never loses sight of where he is going.

IX

Christ As One Avatar:

FORSTER'S
Passage to India

THE only other
modern writer besides Faulkner who impresses me as
having a comparable relativistic and anthropological approach is E. M. Forster. His *Passage to India* (1924) is
at first glance a novel of social comment now somewhat
outdated by the recent turn of events in India, but at a
more sensitive reconsideration a novel making a universal
point through the conscious employment of multi-
cultural rituals and meanings. The several levels of symbolic meaning may be suggested through a brief tracing
of Mrs. Moore, an English woman visiting in India. On
her visit to her son Ronnie, a physician in the colonial
service, she is accompanied by Miss Quested, a fellow
country-woman and her son's fiancée. Mrs. Moore enters
the book in the pleasantly cool weather after the rainy
season. She goes in the moonlight to a mosque, where her
respect for the Moslem custom of removing one's shoes
before entering sacred ground, her willingness to accept
the Moslems as her equals, and the expressions that "God
is Love" and "God is Everywhere" win her the admira-

tion and devotion of the young Moslem Aziz, similarly
a physician working for the English government. Like
a Hindu she feels at one with the wasp, a creature considered under Hinduism as worthy of respect as man
himself but showing no respect for the unnatural,
ephemeral bounds of a man-built house. From the position of a sincere Christian she criticizes the discrimina-
tory and disciplinary policies of the English civil serv-
ants who sing "God Save the King" without believing
in either God or the King. She functions as a kind of
goddess-ideal in each of the three designated religious
contexts. This first section of the novel in which Mrs.
Moore evolves so admirably according to several points
of view is entitled "The Mosque." Here the reader is
given a picture of the Moslem as Western-educated,
self-consciously rational yet full of superstition and suspicion, too sophisticated for intense religion yet nostalgic
for the political and religious domination of India by the
early Mohammedans. Among the Moslems the emotional
Aziz constantly praises Mrs. Moore as the ideal of love
and understanding.

In section two, "The Cave," in the intensely increasing heat of India comparable in effect to the chilling
cold of the Western winter, Mrs. Moore and Miss
Quested visit a Jainist cave in the company of Aziz and
his native party. Reflected in the darkness of the cave
Mrs. Moore sees the transience and puniness of Man and
hears every sound—"Hope, politeness, the blowing of a
nose, the squeak of a boot"—reduced to the nonsense
nothingness of "boum." Christianity, Mohammedanism,
Hinduism bicker in a mad trial in which Aziz is falsely
accused of affronting Miss Quested in a cave. Miss
Quested ultimately withdraws her unfounded charge,

but not until the hatreds that make up Forster's India have been increased to a kind of white-hot heat quite in keeping with the weather. Mrs. Moore, who in the previous section was an all-pervading goddess of love common to all religions, in this section becomes the voice of the absolute nothingness of creation. She wants only to be let alone and leaves India just when she might help Aziz, who has all but deified her. Ironically at the very moment when she dies en route to England and is buried at sea, the Hindus, celebrating their New Year, ignorantly pick up her name from its mention at the trial of Aziz and chant it mistakenly as "Esmiss Esmoor." They celebrate her as some goddess of the new instead of as an old woman who has actually experienced her winter (in India's heat) of no belief, of the refusal of moral and social responsibility, and of absolute death without promise. Ironically, too, the English and Mohammedans participating in the trial call on her as well as the Hindus, all in their own mistaken and foolish ways. But Forster has repeatedly suggested in one context or another that the god called does not answer. The question of course is whether the god or goddess will be resurrected in the rainy season that follows the death-dealing heat in which Mrs. Moore became the chief Nothing in all-encompassing Nothingness.

In the final section, "The Temple," Esmiss Esmoor enters the consciousness of a Westernized Brahman, Professor Godbole, at the very moment when he is participating in native dress in a festival celebrating the birth of Krishna. In the Hindu religion Krishna is the most popular incarnation (recall Faulkner's "avatars") of the god Vishnu, the Preserver in the trinity along with Brahma the Creator and Siva the Destroyer. Forster mocks the Hindu ritual in a variety of ways: Godbole's pince-nez becomes mixed up in the leis of flowers around his neck; the rajah's scrawny band imitates Western marches in the courtyard; and the rajah himself, who is supposed to represent Krishna in the festival, is dead though the people do not know it, just as Mrs. Moore was dead when the Hindus called her in the previous section. As in *Light in August* the chief correlative of Christ is handled repeatedly to suggest the similar patterns of other religions, in *Passage to India* the story of Krishna is related to that of Christ:

In a land where all else was unpunctual, the hour of the Birth was chronometrically observed. Three minutes before it was due, a Brahman brought forth a model of the village of Gokul (the Bethlehem in that nebulous story) and placed it in front of the altar. The model was on a wooden tray about a yard square; it was of clay, and was gaily blue and white with streamers and paint. Here, upon a chair too small for him and with a head too large, sat King Kansa, who is Herod, directing the murder of some Innocents, and in a corner, similarly proportioned, stood the father and mother of the Lord, warned to depart in a dream. The model was not holy, but more than a decoration, for it diverted men from the actual image of the God, and increased their sacred bewilderment.

The ceremony in which the crèche plays such an important part ends in the annihilation of sorrow, of disease, of "doubt, misunderstanding, cruelty, fear," or at least the "books written afterwards" say as much. Forster throws in a joker of considerable size: the believer "may think, if he chooses, that he has been with God, but as soon as he thinks it, it becomes history, and falls under the rules of time." In any case, the rains do come, the waters overflow, and all of the main characters on hand, including two children of Mrs. Moore, in attitude not unlike their mother in section one, are dunked gleefully in the river. One may recall the hilarious meeting of Lena and Byron at the end of *Light in August*, but in *Passage to India* there has been no intensely-treated sacrifice like that of Christmas as a pivotal part of the book. Mrs. Moore's death has been pictured as a hopeless finality. Aziz, the Moslem who has constantly sought love, and Fielding, an Englishman once a professional humanitarian and now a professional civil servant, are left bickering about Anglo-Indian relations.

Against the Indian background of the book Mrs. Moore may remind us of Kali, the Mother Goddess of India. Kali is worshipped as the universal mother and the foe of all sinful people. This is conspicuously the function of Mrs. Moore in the first part of the novel, and her death at the point when she is most needed to effect peace and justice may not be so much a comment on her failure as a criticism of the failure of people to pay respect to what she symbolizes. Another novel by Forster, *Howards End*, uses the correlative of the universal mother figure in various and wonderful ways. Here, more hopefully, though involvement in the conscious world makes us forget the Source of Life from which we came, the proper sacrifices bring the dead mother back to earth again. The conspicuous mythic analogy of *Howards End* is the body of stories revolving around Demeter, particularly that of Demeter and Persephone. Forster subtly and yet strikingly interweaves these analogies with others from Plato, Goethe, Homer, and the Bible, and reminds us among other things that though each culture may dramatize its needs distinctively, the needs are basically the same and peculiar dramatizations are implicitly universal. In the novels which we have examined, especially Sonia (*Crime and Punishment*) and Lena (*Light in August*) evolve as the archetypal woman, virgin-mate-mother, in positive ways, though the center of the drama remains the archetypal male who acts out the play of death-and-resurrection. In *Passage to India* Mrs. Moore has similar potentialities of nursing mankind from its illness to a wholeness of spirit, but she does not fulfill them and becomes sort of a mock figure. Still, Forster's tone wishes that she had achieved her traditional purpose as after a great deal of struggle he allows Margaret to do in *Howards End*.

I have mentioned Forster as a writer with the anthropological and mythic sense of Faulkner, enabling him to see Christ as one symbol of the death-resurrection juxtaposition that occurs in every religion. The mock or inverse way in which Forster employs his religious frame of reference in *Passage to India* is much closer in tone to the futility of *Soldier's Pay* and *Sartoris*, though nearer in technique to the richness of *Light in August*, to mention only those books by Faulkner arbitrarily chosen for my purpose. In *Light in August* Faulkner may continue to condemn the varieties of institutional Christianity, but he presents positively the primitive Christians' values of sacrifice and love. The fruitless calling of the god and final mockery are characteristic of many novels of the 1920's when *Soldier's Pay*, *Sartoris*, and *Passage to India* were all written. The "false dawn" which Mrs. Moore and Miss Quested experience as they move in India's heat to a crisis in which hate is expanded reminds one of Hemingway's "false spring" in *A Farewell to Arms* when Lieutenant Henry and Catherine

Barkley enter the supposed haven of neutral Switzerland. There Catherine and her child are to die, leaving
Lieutenant Henry to walk in terrible loneliness "back to
the hotel in the rain." And even earlier Jake Barnes in
The Sun Also Rises is no more successful in overcoming
his emasculation than the implicit Fisher King in Eliot's
Waste Land or the symbolically dead protagonist in
Soldier's Pay. By the end of the 'twenties, in such works
as *The Sound and the Fury*, and certainly by the early
'thirties when *Light in August* appeared, Faulkner may
have been well on the way to the body of belief which
he later presented so dramatically in book after book.
Yet *Light in August* and *Passage to India*, however much
more mocking Forster may have been in his approach,
agree that Christ-Krishna is a spring god which Calvinist prototypes forget in their emphasis on abnegation. At
the same time that he is amused at Hinduism, Forster at
least grants it this much: "By sacrificing good taste, this
worship achieved what Christianity has shirked: the inclusion of merriment." Whatever the later books suggest in their increasingly orthodox emphasis, Faulkner
seems to agree in *Light in August* that Christianity without merriment is no Christianity at all.

If the novels of Faulkner and Forster discussed
above may be read superficially as social comments, their
unity and structure are clear only in terms of their
religious and/or mythic patterns. In each book the in-
humanity of man is part of the denial of love, but love
must be intuitively, mystically, naïvely expressed by
individuals if it is to dispel the personal hate and social
prejudice that make up the winter of the world. In
Light in August Miss Burden, who makes it her New
England, Calvinist, abolitionist *duty* to receive Negroes

as equals and to try to improve them through *education*, is the foil of sterility to Lena Grove's innocent fertility. And in *Passage to India* Miss Quested, who wants so much to see the "real India," is not really concerned about "real Indians" and brings tremendous trouble to the native characters of the novel. Fielding, who is a kind of professional do-gooder, incurs ultimately the distrust of Aziz, the Moslem on whose behalf he opposed the entire English colony, and he develops into a kind of busybody deputy for English schools throughout India. To neither Faulkner nor Forster is group action for social ends a Christ-like endeavor. In *Intruder in the Dust* (1948), Faulkner insists that the South will work out its problems not through legislation but through individual courage and individual changes of heart, and in *Passage to India* Forster, without even hope in the individual, leaves us with the feeling that justice may be included along with "Hope, politeness, the blowing of a nose, the squeak of a boot" as one of the noises which produce after all only "boum."

BIBLIOGRAPHICAL NOTE:

COMPARATIVE RELIGION

A single reminder of Christ through Krishna may hardly seem sufficient reason for considering Forster's *Passage to India*, but here is an excellent example of a Western writer's inability to keep Christ out of his Eastern setting and frame of reference. More properly one may pursue here the concept of a sacrificing or sacrificed Mother rather than that of sacrificial hero. Look back toward our references to Sonia in *Crime and Punishment* and ahead to those to Cristina in *Bread and Wine*. But look more fruitfully, again, at Kerenyi and Jung's *Essays on a Science of Mythology* (New York, 1949) and at the endlessly exciting *The Great Mother: An Analysis of the Archetype* by Erich Neumann (New York, 1955). My reference to Mrs. Wilcox in *Howards End* is the center of an article by me, "A New Correlative for 'Howards End': Demeter and Persephone" (The Lock Haven *Bulletin*, Pennsylvania State College, 1961), one of a series of exercises in "name-calling." The previous chapter on Faulkner is in some ways indulgence in this popular critical game as is my article "*The Age of Innocence:* Edith Wharton's Weak Faust" (*College English*, December, 1959). For fuller discussions of Eastern religions see John C. Archer's *The Sikhs in Relation to Hindus, Moslems, Christians, and Ahmadiyyas* (Princeton, 1946), Eli S. Jones' *Christ at the Round Table* (New York, 1928), and Paul Thomas' *Hindu Religions, Customs, and Manners* (Bombay, 1956). Of special interest is Max Weber's *The Religion of India: The Sociology of Hinduism and Buddhism* (translated and edited by Hans H. Gerth and Don Martindale, Glencove, Illinois, 1958).

X

Christ As The Brother Of Man:

STEINBECK'S
Grapes of Wrath

BY contrast one thinks of the proletarian novels of the 'thirties in which group action, sacrifice for a cause, hope in the future, etc. are treated with considerable respect. The economic determinism implicit in so much of proletarian fiction has often been criticized as a surface matter, naïvely materialistic in emphasis and totally secular in orientation. But many of these novels accented their faith, social or otherwise, with a clear-cut use of religious imagery and Biblical story patterns. The great American novel of this group and of this period is of course Steinbeck's *The Grapes of Wrath*, which I find retains its original power despite the current fashion of decrying Mr. Steinbeck's versatile talent and established significance. The critics have constantly referred to *The Grapes of Wrath* as a naturalistic novel, but naturalism with a difference: Malcolm Cowley, for example, once called it naturalistic in "all but the hortatory passages," suggesting the familiar dichotomy between a theoretically scientific, detached naturalism and an intense faith in and

hope for the peoples of the earth. As a matter of fact,
although Steinbeck has elsewhere treated these attitudes
as opposing sets of values between which the artist must
choose, through Casy he shows very dramatically how
one attitude can develop out of or replace the other.

In the beginning Casy is a preacher in the institutional sense of the word: he uses words in the pulpit
to bring his congregation to grace, he tells them what
is good and warns them against what is bad, he administers the ritual of baptism. But he recognizes that
he himself denies by his actions the very words he employs and that no amount of praying, of word-magic,
will keep him from doing so. In his own words: "I was
a damned ol' hypocrite. But I didn't mean to be." Casy
has discovered the discrepancy between the pretense of
religion and the actuality of the people, and he finds
it impossible to carry out the pretense any longer. This
recognition and this rejection have occurred before the
story begins, and when we first see Casy, he has become
in many ways the naturalist, free of the pretenses of
society, yet without the faith which is so necessary to
the existence of man. He says of fornicating: "Maybe
it ain't a sin. Maybe it's just the way folks is. Maybe
we been whippin' the hell out of ourselves for nothin',"
and of his language: "Maybe you wonder about me
using bad words. Well, they ain't bad to me no more.
They're jus' words folks use, an' they don't mean
nothing bad with 'em." Or more generally and more
significantly: "Law changes, but 'got to's' go on. You
got the right to do what you got to do." His speech at
the grave of Grandpa is everything the institutional
prayer is not. "This here ol' man jus' lived a life and jus'
died out of it. I don't know whether he was good or

bad, but that don't matter much. He was alive, and that's what matters." The stolid Ma approvingly describes him: "That preacher, he's gettin' roun' to thinkin' that what people does is right to do."

Casy has substituted for the absolute morality of institutional religion the relative morality of naturalism, but this professedly "scientific" position proves to be simply a step from the pretense of faith by words to an even greater faith in the Word which can be put into action. "Maybe it's all men and women we love; maybe that's the Holy Spirit—the human spirit—the whole shebang. Maybe all men got one big soul everybody's a part of," he says again and again in the best transcendentalist tradition, and in the best Marxist tradition he accepts the necessity for organization and the gradual working out of the dialectic as "as natural as rain." Steinbeck has richly dramatized Casy's throwing off of the false Christianity and, via the road of naturalism, his arrival at the true religion which consists of strong transcendental and Marxist elements, perhaps even Christianity before its corruption. The development of Casy makes him a walking history of ideas for the first three decades of twentieth-century America, and implicitly a symbol for that part of it which we call literary history.

Reconsider for a moment the previously mentioned lament of Krutch that the soul, hence faith, hence tragedy, had become dead ducks by 1929. In the historically important *Modern Temper* of that year, the book in which Mr. Krutch's lament was so eloquently presented, Humanism and Nature were described as "fundamentally antithetical." Sadly enough, Krutch could only conclude: "if we no longer believe in either our infinite

capacities or our importance to the universe, we know
at least that we have discovered the trick which has
been played upon us and that whatever else we may be we
are no longer dupes." "Ours is a lost cause," he wrote
in the concluding sentence to his book, "and there is
no place for us in the natural universe, but we are not,
for all that, sorry to be human. We should rather die
as men than live as animals." If Conrad's dualistic man,
say, was anachronistically an eighteenth-century concept, Krutch wishes that his psychology could be. He
speaks very clearly as the nineteenth-century liberal who
knows too much; he is conditioned to the values of
orthodox dualism which evolve from a belief in the
Reasoning Man who has a choice and will choose for
the public good, but he sees these very values denied by
the new science on which the intellectual cannot turn
his back. Having lamented that our scientific destruction
of individualism made us incapable of either conceiving
or understanding tragedy, Krutch came ironically close
to sounding like a twentieth-century Hamlet, taught a
set of values his intellectual self could no longer accept,
yet without an intellectual climate in which he could
live sincerely and effectively. The irony may be, as Mr.
Krutch suggests in quite different terms, that tragedy of
the individual can be understood and expressed only in
the transition from the myth of authority (for example,
medievalism) to the myth of individualism, and not in
the transition from the myth of individualism to the
myth of authority (socialism, or if one likes, a return to
medievalism). In the former the individual may be
driven to physical catastrophe, but he transcends this
catastrophe by his very discovery of himself as an individual. In the latter the individual is likewise physically

crushed, but he pathetically knows that considering himself an individual has been after all "words, words, words," for science tells him that he is otherwise.

One is apt to dismiss Mr. Krutch's dilemma as the culmination of the post-war disillusionment which dominated the literature of the 1920's, and point to the social consciousness of the 1930's as something else again, as a kind of chorus of survival after the chorus of despair. Still, the logical problem of making compatible intellectual naturalism and intellectual humanism remains. Most intellectuals who came of age before 1945 were naturalists enough to demand verifiable transitions, to be leery of faith even when they felt it naturally. To the conscious analyst the climate of opinion of the past develops into, is not superseded by, the climate of opinion of the present.

Coming at the end of the 1930's, just as *The Modern Temper* came at the end of the 'twenties, there appeared in *The New Republic* between January and October, 1939, a series of articles entitled "Books That Changed Our Minds," written by such distinguished men of letters as Lewis Mumford, Charles Beard, David Daiches, Max Lerner, Bernard Smith. The books discussed in the series had been selected on the basis of a poll of all living *New Republic* contributors and included the works of Spengler, Dewey, Frederick J. Turner, Parrington, I. A. Richards, Henry Adams, Veblen, Boas, Charles Beard, Sumner, Freud, and Lenin (the list was restricted to twentieth-century books; hence, Marx and Darwin, for example, were omitted). The series was significant as a statement of intellectual influence in a magazine considered since its founding an important journal of liberal opinion. Malcolm Cowley, who later edited the series in book form, summarized the implications of the articles as follows:

One result of fitting the studies together is the utter destruction of the Reasoning Man. John Stuart Mill had portrayed him as possessing certain attributes: he was rational, he was civilized, he was morally free, he was an individual. Now, one by one, these attributes had been stripped away from him. He was not rational; on the contrary, most of his actions were conditioned reflexes and many of them were the acting out in symbolic form of suppressed desires; his psychology could best be understood by studying that of animals or children. He was not civilized; on the contrary, his social behavior was full of concealed survivals from barbarism and was capable of reverting at the least excuse to forthright savagery. He was not morally free, except within a limited sphere; on the contrary, he was subject to his biological nature, to his physical environment, to his class loyalties, to a whole series of laws the existence of which had not even been suspected in the early nineteenth century. And finally, he was not even an individual, in the sense that Mill had used the word, since his life as a human being was inseparable from his social life. Unless he belonged to a community, he was deprived of his human heritage, he was a beast among beasts.

On the surface this concept of man is without faith and without hope, and it is especially remarkable that it should be implicit in the books that influenced most strongly the contributors to a magazine that constantly asks the application of reason to the affairs of man, that assumes man is worth helping, that insists further that man can be helped in every crisis if every reader does what he can. Here again is the dichotomy of Nature and Humanism. But whereas Krutch in 1929 concluded that the Nature of the modern climate of opinion destroyed effective Humanism, *The New Republic* seems somehow naturalistic and humanistic at once.

The juxtaposition of the naturalists' rather dismal picture of man and society and of the liberals' hopeful picture has not been and is not uncommon. Frank Norris in such a pioneering work as *The Octopus* (1901) could write on one page: "Men were naught, life was naught —Force only existed" and twenty pages later: "The individual suffers, but the race goes on. . . . The larger view always and through all shams, all wickedness discovers the Truth that will, in the end, prevail." Upton Sinclair in *The Jungle* (1905) could move suddenly from Jurgis, beaten in body and in spirit by men expressing their basic animalism, particularly men in a capitalist society, to Jurgis inspired by socialism, "the new religion of humanity—or you might say it was the fulfillment of the old religion, since it implied the literal application of all the teachings of Christ." Even Dreiser, as early as *An American Tragedy*, before his confusing combination of mysticism and Communism, presents Clyde Griffiths, when hope is gone almost entirely from Clyde and even more completely from the reader, as the source and means of a growing spirituality and strength of character, forced to pay a penalty to the state not alone for his own weakness but for the weaknesses of an entire system. These artists feel no need to relate logically their intense naturalism and the accompanying optimism, whether it is Emersonian transcendentalism, Christian socialism, or a belief in tragedy. As novelists, they are concerned not with logic, but with social realism and psychological probability.

Krutch, however, could not be content to admit intellectually Darwin, Freud, and other nineteenth- and twentieth-century forces and at the same time to believe emotionally in the goodness of man and in the movement of society toward increasing democratization. Acknowledging naturalism, he had to lament the death of humanism, just as Conrad earlier proclaiming his faith in man's greatness of soul could do so only by a rejection of modern naturalistic thought. Critics and scholars, they of the ordered minds, can sympathize: to conclude with Cowley and *The New Republic* that Reasoning Man is dead is rationally to demand that all feelings expressing a love for and a belief in man be re-evaluated in terms of the pathetic rather than the tragic framework.

But Casy was no scholar, and Steinbeck is after all a novelist. Casy's development from orthodoxy to amoral naturalism to belief in the holiness of man and the immortality of mankind is dramatically convincing. The argument of his change is, as it should be, experiential rather than philosophical.

The total pattern of *The Grapes of Wrath* keeps directing us toward a new and truer religion, or—if one likes—Christianity resurrected. There is not only the Biblical style, but on the one hand the Old Testament story of the dispossessed people, the trek through the wilderness, literally a desert, with its starvation and its death, the promised land, peoples who have decayed with their unnatural wealth, and the sustaining hope in the future; and on the other, the New Testament narrative of the leader who goes into the wilderness, learns the truth which is the love of men, lives among the people, begins to teach them the light at the risk of his own life, is crucified by the deputies of those who own the land and rule it, and dies, leaving behind him a disciple who will devote his life to spreading the Word.

If Casy is strikingly Christ with Tom Joad as the disciple he leaves behind, he is a Christ whose sacrifice is almost a strategy to get people so angry that they keep fighting and keep believing that they *must* win their fight. In *In Dubious Battle*, written three years before *The Grapes of Wrath*, when Steinbeck was more conspicuously working out the conflict of the artist as scientific observer (Dr. Burton) and the artist as participant (Mac and Jim), the organizer Mac drags the body of his co-worker and friend Jim before the crowd, sets it up in the proper place and light, and speaks the final sentence of the book: "This guy didn't want nothing for himself—" The step to a novel such as *The Grapes of Wrath* developing fully another "guy who didn't want nothing for himself" and eliminating the naturalistic Dr. Burton except as a stage in the guy's development is an easy one, but Steinbeck adds still another dimension to his sacrificing, and sacrificed, protagonist. Casy says to the man who strikes him his fatal blow, "You don't know what you're a-doin'." "Jesus, George," a second deputy exclaims with an unwitting pun, "I think you killed him." Then like a light thrown on a crucifix, "the flashlight beam dropped, searched, and found Casy's crushed head." A point of difference from the Scriptures is Tom's immediate fighting response instead of the familiar denial of Christ by even the apostles.

An unchanging figure in *The Grapes of Wrath* is Ma Joad, who acts as an impressive sustenance throughout the travails that come to man and his land. Men live in jerks, women in flows, she tells us, and she flows her encouragement and persistence throughout the novel, somehow intuitively knowing that mankind is One, that there is protection in union, that the people will live on.

In *To a God Unknown* Steinbeck revealed an extensive acquaintance with the great fertility myths, and Ma Joad is certainly a kind of mother-earth-fertility goddess accompanying and continuing beyond Casy's crucifixion and Tom's mission, just as Faulkner's Lena Grove continues beyond Christmas' death. The transcendental Oneness of mankind and the social power of organized strike become an enlarged family sense in her vast female consciousness. Earlier in the novel, Ma Joad feels and knows that survival of the Joads depends on her keeping the literal family together, but by the end of the book when the family of man has formulated in her awareness, she can let Tom go literally and still have him spiritually.

The themes of Christ and the fertility goddess are brought together in the somewhat sensational final scene of the book. The actual remnant of the Joad family, directed by Ma, has fled from a flood to take shelter in a barn into which it has trespassed. There the significantly named Rose of Sharon, deserted by her husband and recovering from the birth of her dead child, suckles a dying old man, as, Madonna-like, she "smiled mysteriously." Casy's death of course has given the Joads new strength, and the last scene points up that a man has died so that Man may live.

Although Steinbeck's treatment of Casy is more complicated, the essence of Christ implicit in every leader of the working man is vividly portrayed in "Jesus Christ," a song recorded by Woody Guthrie, the balladeer. Incidentally, the album in which the song is included with five others by Guthrie, has a foreword by Steinbeck. In the preface he says, among other things, "A few years ago when I sat in the camps of the people

from the dustbowl when hunger was everywhere, I heard
the singing and I knew that this was a great race, for,
while there was loneliness and trouble in the singing,
there was also fierceness and a will to fight," and of
Guthrie specifically, in his singing "is the will of a people to endure and fight against oppression . . . the American spirit." Guthrie's Jesus is a "hard working Man . . . a
Carpenter by trade," who travels through the land, ad-
vising the rich "to give your goods to the poor."

When Jesus came to town, the working folks around,
Believed what He did say:
The bankers and the preachers they nailed him on a cross,
And they laid Jesus Christ in His Grave.
Poor working people, they follered him around,
Sung and shouted gay;
Cops and the soldiers they nailed him on a cross,
And they laid Jesus Christ in His Grave.

Both Steinbeck's and Guthrie's Christs are what Empson would call a version of the pastoral in their reversal of
the traditional low and the traditional high, one version of
course having been specifically designated by Empson as
proletarian art. The pastoral implications are compounded
in Guthrie's final lines, so derogatory of the metropolis:

This song was written in New York City,
Of rich men, preachers, and slaves;
If Jesus was to preach like he preached in Galilee,
They would lay Jesus Christ in his grave.

The Christ figure of the 'thirties is in the last analysis a kind of melodramatic, if moving, hero who represents the potential goodness in man. There is little emphasis on his playing the part of scapegoat for the follies
of the people who deny him his savior function, as for

example there is in Faulkner's Christmas, who is for a
while all evil and who must be sacrificed for a rejuvenation of those related to him. Casy's death may not have
occurred if the workers, even though hungry, had completely supported him in the strike that he preached, but
Steinbeck's attention is considerably less to the failures
of the people than to the increased strength which they
achieve through Casy's martyrdom.

BIBLIOGRAPHICAL NOTE:

THE CLIMATE OF A DECADE

Most of this discussion of Steinbeck was first presented to
the Literature and Society Section of the Modern Language Association, New York, 1947, on a panel of papers on "Contemporary Naturalism." Charles Child Walcutt, author of *American Literary Naturalism: A Divided Stream* (Minneapolis, 1956), presided over the
panel. Other participants were Ralph Gilbert Ross, "Contemporary
Naturalism and the Arts," and Richard Benson Sewall, "Philosophical
and Literary Limitations of Contemporary Naturalism." My paper
was entitled "Naturalism and the Liberal's Dilemma." Malcolm Cowley's famous article on naturalism, recognizing a dichotomy not unlike that pointed to on the panel and in Walcutt's book, was " 'Not
Men': A Natural History of American Naturalism," *Kenyon Review*
(Summer, 1947). Ten years after Krutch's *The Modern Temper*
(New York, 1929), the series on "Books That Changed Our Minds"
appeared in *The New Republic* between January and October, 1939.
Their authors and titles are worth listing because these include some
of the great critics and the great works of our time: Lewis Mumford
on Spengler's *The Decline of the West* (1918), C. E. Ayres on
Dewey's *Democracy and Education* and *Essays in Experimental Logic*
(1916), Charles A. Beard on Turner's *The Frontier in American History* (1890, 1932), Bernard Smith on Parrington's *Main Currents of
American Thought* (1927-1931), David Daiches on Richards' *Principles of Literary Criticism* (1924), Louis Kronenberger on Adams'
own *The Education of Henry Adams* (1918), R. G. Tugwell on

Veblen's *The Theory of the Leisure Class* (1899) and *The Theory of Business Enterprise* (1904), Paul Radin on Boas' *The Mind of Primitive Man* (1911), Max Lerner on Beard's *An Economic Interpretation of the Constitution* (1927), John Chamberlain on Sumner's *Folkways* (1907), George Soule on Freud's *Interpretation of Dreams* (1900), Max Lerner also on Lenin's *The State and Revolution* (1915). (Lenin was included instead of Marx because the list was limited to twentieth-century works.) In the same year the articles appeared as a book, edited by Bernard Smith and Malcolm Cowley, who had summarized their implications in "The End of Reasoning Man." The album of Woody Guthrie's songs to which I refer is *Woody Guthrie* (Ash Recordings, New York, ca. 1943—no date given). Since the 1930's so-called intellectuals have paid serious and popular attention to folksingers, and more recently there has been a striking revival of interest in singers who, in the Guthrie tradition, are for peace, brotherhood, and social sacrifice. Pete Seeger is an example of one such singer. This revival is inspired primarily on the international scene by the bomb and on the home front by the contest over segregation-integration in the South. Perhaps part and parcel of the same revival, Steinbeck and the Depression have begun to replace Fitzgerald and the 'Twenties as a center of concern in some literary magazines and in such indicators of the non-academic intellectual climate of opinion as *Esquire*.

NOTE: Since my comments on Steinbeck were written, he has of course received the Nobel Prize as a kind of grand climax to the revival which I mention, but some academic critics are still resisting admission of his effectiveness.

XI

Christ As Marxist Variant:

SILONE'S
Bread and Wine,

MALRAUX'
Man's Fate,

AND

KOESTLER'S
Darkness at Noon

A DIRECT after-
math of the proletarian novel and the forerunner of a
more recent kind of fiction describing journeys of self-
discovery is the autobiographical novel or literal auto-
biography written usually by ex-members of the Communist Party. The best example of this genre pertinent to
our general discussion is *Bread and Wine* by Ignazio
Silone, the Italian novelist. As is characteristic of this
group of novelists, though he is renouncing the social
movement in connection with which he did much of his
earlier writing, Silone continues to employ the techniques of the proletarian novel: a broad backdrop of
working people, in this case peasants, an abundance of

folk anecdotes, almost documentary picturization of social conditions, occasional dialectic at the expense of
drama.

The dialectic at the core of *Bread and Wine* takes
the form of a dialogue, sometimes spoken, sometimes
conjectured and recorded in a notebook, between Spina,
the revolutionary, and Cristina, the would-be nun of an
aristocratic family. Spina as a student in a church school
was inspired by the teachings of the priest Don Benedetto, who preaches that "the gift of life . . . is spent for
others it enriches and beautifies." Even as a young man
Spina wrote: "I should like, ignoring the consequences,
in every hour of my life to live and struggle for that
which seems to me right and good." By way of attaining
this ideal, he worked throughout Europe in presumably
the Communist Internationale, but came to doubt the
morality of undesirable means for a desirable end, to suspect social theory as unrelated to the needs of the people,
to fear within the Party a bureaucracy as strict as that of
Fascist Italy from which he had fled. It is at that point of
disenchantment that the reader first meets Pietro Spina,
old in countenance (actually disfigurement by way of
disguise upon his return to Italy), tired, sick, but young
in body, "stretched on the straw" between "a row of
rolls" and "a bottle of red wine." This is conspicuously
the moment of the death of the unquestioning revolutionary and the rebirth of Peter the Thorn in a manger
surrounded by the symbolic bread and wine. From then
on, Spina is a kind of non-supernatural Christ. He is full
of kindness and understanding for those whom traditional morality and manners condemn. "Miracles" and
wisdom are imposed upon him by a superstitious, ignorant, oppressed, but unbeatable and humorously suspi-

cious peasantry. He recognizes and humbly identifies himself with apathy, fear, sordidness, and in general the betrayal of others. His growing list of disciples and opponents includes a Magdalene, priests, government deputies, various Judases.

Spina's development into a highly traditional Christ occurs through his relations with a number of specific characters. Cristina is attached to the orthodox ideals of the perfect God, of salvation after the enduring life, of patience with one's lot in this world, in direct opposition to Spina's assumptions of the burdens of man and his belief in social action. In Marxist terms she is the thesis of the old religion, and Spina is the antithesis that forms the new. In their conscious dialectic a synthesis evolves, combining her traditional statement of morality with his revolutionary principles of sacrificial action. In religious terms, Spina is the Christ who is both God and Man, and Cristina is the Holy Ghost above and apart from man. The third member of the Trinity, the God to both Spina and Cristina, is Don Benedetto, who enables the other two to combine their beliefs.

Don Benedetto makes two important points. One of these must give heart to any believer in social action: "In times of conspiratorial and secret struggle the Lord is obliged to hide Himself and assume pseudonyms. . . . Might not the ideal of social justice that animates the masses today be one of the pseudonyms the Lord is using to free Himself from the control of the churches and banks?" His other point must give heart to the doubter of the Party which has disappointed his social faith: "I am convinced that it would be a waste of time to show a people of intimidated slaves a different manner of speaking, a different manner of gesticulating; but perhaps it would be worth while to show them a different way of living. No word and no gesture can be more persuasive than the life, and, if necessary, the death, of a man who strives to be free, loyal, just, sincere, disinterested; a man who shows what a man can be." Dramatically speaking, Spina of course is this ideal Man-God who sets the example and makes the necessary sacrifice.

But the religious symbolism of Silone is not altogether simple. Silone allows no character a single function. Spina is implicitly Peter and Paul and even Judas as well as Christ, Don Benedetto the Lord is at other times the Christ figure, Cristina is the Virgin as well as the Holy Ghost as well as finally a female Christ, Murica the Judas is the potentiality of sin and of penance in every man and finally both a mock and a true Christ, and so on down to comparatively minor characters. There is a kind of Biblical tapestry woven around the threefold, though separate, crucifixion of the characters who make up Silone's Trinity. As they approach each other in conscious moral position, they become in effect one, and all of them must be sacrificed as the example for man. A symbol of the ascension grows out of a kind of ambiguity at the end of the book when Cristina, pursuing the fleeing Spina over the thorn-like rocks of the mountain, cannot discover his footprints in the snow over which he has certainly passed. Perhaps he has been killed by the wolves bearing down upon her, or there is the promise that he has escaped to continue his help of man, or he has literally transcended the earth on which he walked: death and no death, defeat and no defeat at once.

The unifying thread in Silone's symbolically religious tapestry is of course the recurrent reference to bread and wine. The people who make up the back-

ground eat and drink throughout, sustaining themselves
with the productions of their fields and their vineyards,
living literally on the crops of the earth into which their
toil and sweat, their fears and hopes have gone, as if figuratively devouring themselves and the things they are
attached to around them. Spina is fed by them, feeds
with them, and feeds them by the very example of his
life. He breaks bread and drinks with them, for example,
on the occasion of Murica's funeral when the reader is
reminded that it takes nine months to make a man, to
grow the grain, to grow the grapes, tying together the
equation of the bread and the wine with the flesh and the
blood and recalling the ritualistic devourings of man and
God. Don Benedetto has emphasized the godliness in
every man, and even Murica, the informer, has illustrated
it by his heroic death. Don Benedetto is poisoned by the
very consumption of the representational water and wine
as he celebrates his final mass, ironically mocking the
traditional ritual of the government-controlled church
and illustrating that, though killed, *he* is not dead. Recall
Faulkner's several-time use of the denial of food by
Christmas so long as he is the Antichrist or man's curse
unredeemed, and note too Steinbeck's less consciously
ritualistic use of the refusal or willingness to share food
that one finds throughout *The Grapes of Wrath*. There
is incidentally a part of *The Grapes of Wrath* that appears in *The Long Valley*, a collection of short stories, as
a single piece "Breakfast." Here a solitary worker (Tom
in the novel) walks out of the cold morning upon a
father, a son, a son's wife with a child. The family intuitively offers and shares its food with him. Steinbeck
surrounds the experience with a kind of mysticism: "out
of a sunken memory," he says at the beginning, and

"blazing with light at the eastern skyline," he says at the end of the setting into which the character has walked. His central intelligence claims "some element of great beauty then that makes the rush of warmth when I think of it." Steinbeck's is a less ceremonial communion than Silone's constant bread-and-wine partakings, but nevertheless a communion in the proper sense of the word.

From my description Silone's book may seem more complex, more demanding of the reader than Steinbeck's. I am inclined to think otherwise. Silone's advantage of a culture centered around a high church with a drama and a symbolism of its own on which the writer may draw, often becomes for him a narrative disadvantage. For example, he frequently makes his symbolism stick out like a sore thumb since it is in a way public symbolism, an objective rather than a subjective correlative. Despite conscious use of mythic and religious frameworks, Steinbeck may get more spontaneous response from his readers in the comparative absence of church symbolism to tease constantly our explicating curiosities. The very theme of Silone's book bringing social action and a religious rationale together may demand that he argue in specifically Christian terms that God may hide himself in the revolutionary. Steinbeck illustrates this thesis, too, but he subordinates his argument to his drama.

Another pertinent point Silone argues through Don Benedetto near the beginning of *Bread and Wine*. He is talking to some former students: ". . . the study of Greek tragedy . . . could not help you, to face and understand the obscure tragedy that was about to overwhelm you. . . . Certainly we are no longer victims of that ancient Fate of the Greeks, *Anangke*, Nemesis, but what is this new Fate that prevented you from being what you wanted to be? . . . this destiny that has caused many of you, who were Catholics, to become, first, Nationalists, then Socialists, then Fascists, then advocates of the corporate state, and now . . . Socialists again? What is this new and inexorable demon, this new and ferocious destiny, that has taken the place of the Fate of the ancients and plays with your lives like a drunkard playing with dice?" Silone's question is rhetorical, for the world of *isms* is somehow as elusive as the Greek fates, but he has emphasized that we are not guilty of Krutch's charge of "tragic fallacy." It is not that we are without tragedy; we are simply involved in different elements of it.

If we look back from *Bread and Wine* (1938) to Malraux's *Man's Fate* (1933) and forward to Koestler's *Darkness at Noon* (1941), we discover a dramatic history of the social consciousness of the European intellectual for an entire decade. All three authors were actively involved in the Communist "international revolution." Malraux had a significant part in the Chinese Revolution of 1927, the place and time of *Man's Fate*, and in the Spanish Civil War of 1937. In 1938 he left the Party, but for our purposes it is significant that he was an active member when he wrote *Man's Fate*. Silone had helped to found the Italian Communist Party in 1921 and had been an editor of two of its publications during the following decade. In 1930 he left the Party and lived in Switzerland in exile from Fascist Italy as well as from political activity generally for the next ten years. But he was not finished with political life: in 1940 he accepted the direction of the Foreign Center of the Italian Socialist Party, an organization left of the Italian conservatives but right of his contemporary Communist countrymen. *Bread and Wine* is from the active literary period of his

exile, a time of political expatriation but evidently not of
political indifference. Koestler joined the Party in 1931
and left it in 1938. In the meantime, he had fought in
Spain and suffered imprisonment by Franco, only to be
reimprisoned by the French authorities in 1939. He
escaped from France to join the British Army in 1940.
Darkness at Noon comes at the beginning of a period of
philosophical reconsideration of self, apparent in Koestler's non-fiction as well as his fiction. Koestler's contemplation of his previous existence has been accompanied by a pathetic sense of belonging nowhere in
this our world.

    Bread and Wine is a significant transition between
the action of Malraux' protagonist Kyo and the philosophical reconsideration of Koestler's protagonist Rubashov. Spina, recall, is trying to work out a synthesis of
social action and individual morality. Admittedly, so are
the protagonists of Malraux and Koestler, but in Malraux'
novel one is left with the necessity of action *in spite of*
individual doubts and in Koestler's with the necessity of
a personal identity *beyond* the social context. On the
surface the direction has been from the acceptance of social determinism, that is, from freedom as a recognition
of necessity, to the reaffirmation of the will, that is, to
freedom as a transcendence of necessity. Though their
famous books reflect different stages in their journeys of
learning, each of the writers in question has been through
this development and arrived more or less at the same
place. Too, regardless of the emphasized stand at the
time of writing, each of the novels under discussion
treats the conflict of *fatality*, as Malraux calls it, with the
will.

    In a sense, Malraux emphasizes that the fatality cannot be resisted, but he first examines a variety of ways in which individuals make the attempt at resistance. Frequently, the conflict almost disappears with the classical, and now in a different way existentialist, implication that character *is* destiny, that each man chooses his fatality and must be responsible for it. But there are in effect moral distinctions in the levels of fatality: what one character *must* do is by invidious comparison nearer to freedom than what another character *must* do. The dramatic microcosm of Malraux' social macrocosm includes a French capitalist obsessed with power, a police chief for the capitalist forces obsessed with making others lose their integrity as a kind of perverted revenge for his having lost his own, a decadent Western aristocrat obsessed with playing roles to hide his lack of function in the world, a young terrorist obsessed with the pursuit of death as the supreme orgasm, an Oriental artist obsessed with the creation of calm in the midst of chaos, a philosopher who escapes his inability to translate his ideas into action by the smoking of opium. In this, his Communist period, Malraux' imagery is as free of traditional religious imagery as was the style of Turgenev when he was trying to convey the nihilism of his protagonist Bazarov; but as in Turgenev the orthodox patterns nevertheless evolve. The men whose obsessions deny sacrifice for a social cause are surrounded by imagery of the flesh and of death. For Ferral, the capitalist, whose chosen destiny is to manipulate persons for his own satisfaction and power, there is no freedom from the flesh figuratively or literally. His social corruption is reflected in his relationship with the woman Valerie, whom he would like to treat as a piece of property entirely at the mercy of *his* desire. In bed, as in the affairs of the world, he is so egotistical that the art of intercourse is more a kind of masturbation. The concept of the subjected one is as much a part of him as the concept of the ruling individual. Ch'en, the young Communist terrorist, wants to kill Chiang Kai-shek; his rationalization is a social one, but his motivation Malraux makes clear as highly hedonistic. The imagery with which Ch'en is surrounded is, again, that of masturbation and of solitary orgasms.

Malraux has a tremendous capacity for relating the public self and the private self. Like Ferral and Ch'en, Kyo, the main character, demonstrates this capacity. According to his thinking as a young Communist, he believes in the equality of women and grants his wife her "freedom." His wife May, whose fundamental love for Kyo we are not allowed to doubt, goes to bed with a doctor at the hospital where she is also a physician. Kyo's problem is to make his personal response compatible with his belief in an idea, to live by an idea, that is. On a much larger scale, Kyo has worked as an organizer of farm laborers and factory workers; he knows them, and he loves them. He has helped to arm them for participation in the revolution against Chinese feudalism and international capitalism. He knows that Chiang Kai-shek, who has posed as a revolutionary leader carrying out the principles of Sun Yat-sen, is selling out to the opposition for the guarantee of his own power in China. Along this line, Chiang Kai-shek demands the arms of the workers, theoretically to continue the battle on their behalf, actually to liquidate the possibility of achieving the promised communal reforms. Still, the representatives from Moscow in China tell Kyo that there can be no socialist revolution without first the centralization of government characteristic of capitalist revolutions: he must order his

forces to give up the arms now and, as he knows, meet
their deaths as individuals so that all mankind may be
free from death in the future. The conflict between personal love and allegiance to an idea is major for Kyo on
both the sexual and the social level. Loyalty to an idea
demands faith, and the maintenance of faith demands
sacrifice. Kyo keeps this faith in spite of himself: he dies
for the cause to which he is devoted. Freedom from the
flesh, according to Malraux' recurrent imagery, demands
sacrifice of the self. Kyo's father, Old Gisors, the
teacher-philosopher, states that for Kyo, Marxism is
more will than fatality. Kyo's destiny is to be true to the
Marxist idea. Paradoxically, in the *choice* of allegiance
to historical inevitability, Kyo combines individual integrity with social participation.

We have mentioned earlier Lawrence's ironic freedom from physiological determinism in his *worship* of
the body. Similarly, at this point, Malraux finds a freedom from social determinism through the *devotion* to
Marxism. Certainly, Malraux' final evaluation of Kyo is
as a tragic hero dying so that other men may live. The
imagery is hardly Christian: in passing, the failure of all
institutional religion, Christianity explicitly and Buddhism, Confucianism, and Taoism implicitly, is dramatized.
Still, Kyo's pattern is the sacrificial hero's as truly as that
of Spina whom Silone identifies so consciously with
Christ. The prototype of the Communist fighter, Katov,
may seem to some readers to achieve the godhead more
fully: within the scope of the novel he is free of doubt
and indecision, and even in the face of death by torture
he gives his cyanide to the young revolutionaries lying
beside him. But the figure through whom we are purged
must wear one guise, the guise of man. Kyo *is* imperfect,

as the scapegoat must ultimately be when he dies bearing the sins of others. That in the face of torture he commits suicide, Malraux relates to the "honorable" Japanese tradition of hara-kiri. Kyo is "half" Japanese. Along the line of our discussion, would the sacrificial hero of the Japanese kill himself instead of waiting to be crucified by those whom he is trying to help?

One other point: Katov is an older man and an experienced Communist. He is a kind of father figure to Kyo and the others whose experience in revolution is limited to the surrounding Chinese one. But the figure more suggestive of the archetypal father in the great religious dramas is Kyo's actual father, Old Gisors. He is the father of the revolution in that his one-time Hegelian teachings have influenced Ch'en, Kyo, and many other young revolutionaries. But Malraux is highly critical of him as the non-translator of ideas into action and indeed as the fugitive from the real world in his habitual taking of opium. Interestingly enough, though, the god-the-father figures are repeatedly dramatized as Immobile, the Immutable, the Principle-beyond-Action, and the function of savior in the world is left to the son. Remember Stein in *Lord Jim* sitting Buddha-like and sending Jim into a new world to work out the redemption of man. Or even Vassily, the wise old father of *Fathers and Sons*, who cannot stop the working out of the sacrificial pattern in Bazarov. Don Benedetto, to be sure, finally comes out of retirement to share Spina's crucifixion, but even then his death occurs in a church during the performance of the ritualistic mass and not out in the world as does Spina's— pretending for the moment that either of them dies. Long ago in translating the Scriptures into a new dramatic form, Milton had God send out Michael and then of course Christ to *act* in the face of crisis; the Omnipotent and Omniscient can hardly be allowed to *move*. And more recently, Faulkner in *A Fable* faced the same problem of drama with the father, a general in high place, who in effect wills that his natural son, the corporal, *work out* the pattern of redemption. Except for one scene, Old Gisors sits behind the walls of his tasteful house surrounded by Oriental objects of art, including exquisite paintings of the Phoenix, and quietly mouths truths or disappears into the clouds of opium smoke. The revolution goes on around him, and people on all sides in the fight come to him presumably for insight into themselves. In the one scene in which he leaves his isolation, Gisors, unwilling to have Kyo die, goes out to save him, but ineffectually so. Gisors has passed on to Kyo the idea for which Kyo will die, and there is no undoing of his own teaching. According to Malraux' tone, however, Gisors is not *above* action, but incapable of it. Here the god-the-father figure is not irreproachable.

Old Gisors, who starts out as a teacher of political philosophy in China, ends as a teacher of Occidental art in Japan. Temporarily he gives up opium when faced with the actual death of Kyo, but as the book closes he has already returned to his self-indulgent clouds. I mention this as of special interest with respect to Malraux' own development from far left when he wrote *Man's Fate*, to far right as the support of De Gaulle after World War II, to his asocial position more recently as a student of aesthetics who rather professes to have found Truth in a Grecian Urn.

Koestler's Rubashov of *Darkness at Noon* finds Truth deep within the recesses of the heart and mind rather than in any man-created evidences of beauty outside of us. Unlike Kyo acting in a revolution and Spina living among the people, Rubashov is isolated in a Russian prison cell, following his arrest by fellow Communist officials. His journey of learning is chiefly a solitary journey of retrospect and contemplation though each of the main sections of the book ends with his journeying literally and figuratively to face an official judge. As in all true stories of learning, the final judge is himself in more ways than one. The key to the threefold structure of the book Rubashov states in his diary at the beginning of section three, "The Third Hearing." He accepts a kind of cultural lag of the masses in his contention that they will fail for several generations to understand the state of affairs that they themselves have created in the Revolution. Until the masses reach this state of maturity, the opposition can never appeal to their sense of justice as it can do in a working democracy. In "opposition," he is of course including himself, currently under arrest by a faction which demands his liquidation for obscure and elusive reasons. In "periods of mental immaturity" of the masses, such as that dramatized in the novel, "only demagogues invoke the 'higher judgment of the people.'"

The opposition then has three choices. The first is the romantic one of seizing the power by *coup d'état* even without the support of the masses. This Rubashov figuratively attempts when, facing his contemporary Ivanov, who is in charge of the prison, he defiantly claims that he will never admit to the "crimes" of which he is not guilty. "I rebel," he says in effect. The second is "in mute despair . . . to die in silence." Is this, he wonders, what is required of the revolutionary at certain moments of history? Silence is figuratively his response to the investigator Ivanov when the latter, evidently full of guilt and uncertainty, visits Rubashov in his cell rather than having Rubashov make a second journey through the corridors to him. The third choice is "the denial and suppression of one's own conviction when there is no prospect of materializing it." He concludes:

As the only moral criterion which we recognize is that of social utility, the public disavowal of one's conviction in order to remain in the Party's ranks is obviously more honourable than the quixotism of carrying on a hopeless struggle.

Questions of personal pride; prejudices such as exist elsewhere against certain forms of self-abasement; personal feelings of tiredness, disgust and shame—are to be cut off root and branch.

The third choice is dramatized in the public confession which Rubashov makes after his repeated journeys to Gletkin, his final investigator.

Gletkin is the new champion, the man of "correct brutality," "the Neanderthal," whom Rubashov and his generation of intellectual revolutionaries have spawned. It is inevitable that he replace Rubashov, and Rubashov's confession enables the natural continuity of things to evolve. Gletkin will of course get his too, but as the new champion he can learn this only from experience. Gletkin may talk of the utility of scapegoats at certain periods in history and detachedly point to Rubashov as a necessary scapegoat, but like Oedipus answering the Sphinx, he shows no insight into the ultimate applicability of his speech to himself. Rubashov's refrain, "I shall pay," reminds one of Lord Jim's "I take it upon my head" and, to be sure, of Christ's insistence upon crucifixion. The true scapegoat is always "the opposition," an opposition that does not rebel, does not die in desperate silence, but does stand trial for the sins of every man in his time. So Lord Jim did, so Raskolnikov did, so Rubashov does, and so did the Christ of the Scriptures.

Koestler uses the Christ analogies throughout the book. Rubashov expels Richard, a conscientious young man, from the Party into a life of disillusionment and aloneness; the scene takes place in a museum against the background of a drawing of the *Pieta*, which haunts Rubashov throughout his life. Little Loewy hangs himself, Arlova is falsely accused and judged, and Rubashov's guilt takes the form of the traditional Pieta: in the conscious world as the devoted Party member, he uses any means for the desirable end and becomes the crucifier of man for whom the source of life mourns and mourns and mourns. How can it be that allegiance to the "most promising experiment in history" can haunt him as a betrayer of mankind? Loyalty to the conscious world in which one plays a role is, alas, always playing the Judas to humanity. The Antichrist is dramatized through man's involvement in the conscious world; the Christ assumes the form of the scapegoat who admits the evil of the conscious world and takes responsibility for it. Koestler brings together skillfully and movingly the three emphases—first, that any society is the incarnation of Evil on earth; second, that the new champion must die for having been of his world when he becomes the old champion; third, that "one can only be crucified in the name of one's own faith." Recall Stein's advice to Lord Jim: to the destructive element submit! The learning of this essentially religious truth through experience results in a kind of tragic dignity for the "crucified" Rubashov: he comes to understand that despite his physical defeat,

he has his own little place ("the grammatical fiction I")
in the vast order of things ("the oceanic sense").

The denouement of the book counterpoints a news-
paper description of Rubashov's confession with the Biblical narrative of Christ's betrayal and crucifixion. However, when Koestler returns to the actual description of
Rubashov's execution, his final tone assumes a humble
ambivalence:

> Moses had not been allowed to enter the land of
> promise either. But he had been allowed to see it, from the
> top of a mountain, spread at his feet.

Rubashov, who has played the sad fate of every leader
out to its inevitable curtain, wonders why he has not
been taken to the top of the mountain, why he sees
wherever he looks nothing "but desert and the darkness
of night." The title of the book immediately comes to
mind: when Christ was on the cross, "from the sixth
hour [noon] there was darkness all over the land into
the ninth hour," and "about the ninth hour Jesus cried
with a loud voice . . . My God, my God, why hast thou
forsaken me?" But the story does not end there, and perhaps the story of Rubashov has somehow become more
than that of the man of his time. Koestler's final ambivalence reminds us of Marlow's asking after Jim's dramatic
fulfillment of redemption whether Jim's death has been a
significant or a nonsensical one.

That we can conceive of Kyo, the orthodox Communist; Spina, the Christian Marxist; and Rubashov, the
renegade Communist, as analogues of the Christ figure
forcefully emphasizes Don Benedetto's point that in
different times the savior takes different forms. Finding

the analogy in Malraux is simply a recognition of the archetypal pattern of the sacrificial hero. Finding it in Silone is following the explicit reading directions. Finding it in Koestler is following the directions, too, but they are quieter and more uncertain. Perhaps the contemporary intellectual is not far enough away from identification with Rubashov to answer the question about himself: Antichrist or Christ?

BIBLIOGRAPHICAL NOTE:

A HISTORY OF SOCIAL PHILOSOPHY

The changes in social attitude implicit in the three novels discussed are traced provocatively in Edmund Wilson's *To the Finland Station: A Study in the Writing and Acting of History* (New York, 1940). The most pertinent book to my discussion is *The God That Failed* (New York, 1949). Edited by Richard Crossman, M.P. and political theorist, it includes dramatically subjective and recollective essays by "The Initiates," Arthur Koestler, Ignazio Silone, and Richard Wright, and by "Worshipers from Afar," André Gide (presented by Dr. Enid Starkie), Louis Fischer, and Stephen Spender. A pertinent secondary study, R. W. B. Lewis' *The Picaresque Saint* (Philadelphia, 1959), is full of sharp insights, particularly into the total body of Silone's work. For an extremely interesting response to the changing climate of opinion one should look in *Masses and Mainstream* of the late 'forties at essays which reevaluate the earlier praised novels of Malraux after his apparent deviation from the Party. Malraux' writings since his identification with DeGaulle have been primarily in the area of art history and aesthetics (*Voices of Silence*, translated by Stuart Gilbert, Toronto, 1953), reminding one variously of the position of Old Gisors and his painter brother-in-law. These works, it should properly be pointed out, are much more than either art history *or* aesthetics: they reveal a movement toward the kind of mystic sense that characterizes the current climate, furthermore toward a kind of Oriental serenity in the midst of political manipulation and bombings.

XII

Christ As Existentialist Antichrist:

CAMUS'
The Stranger

THE orthodox articulation of faith toward which Silone and Koestler have moved is ironically close in its individualistic imagery to the post-World War II philosophy which Sartre calls atheistic existentialism. Neo-orthodoxy and existentialism both emphasize the freedom of man. Each makes the individual responsible for what he is at the moment, implicitly attacking the climate of opinion of the 'thirties with its awareness of social obligations and its placing of social blame. The differences of the two attitudes are as great as those of, say, Puritanism and hedonism in fundamental assumptions and translation into overt behavior, but in a sense even these traditional opponents are alike in their "strike out for yourself" credos. They are certainly on common ground in their opposition to the Marxist positions of whatever denomination. To the high church, Communism with a small or a capital letter has been the arch-devil. Sartre's classic essay on existentialism, originally a speech delivered at the Sorbonne, is usually printed with a subsequent attack on his pronouncements by a Marxist thinker. That orthodoxy is a moral position and existentialism is by the same standards amoral, does not preclude either from being asocial, so far as overt behavior is concerned. The conservative of the nineteen-thirties charged the New Deal with the destruction of individual freedom and the W.P.A. worker with the sin of sloth, and the status-quo government man of the 'fifties showed suspicion of public works. In the 'thirties similarly, the die-hard writer of the 'twenties who refused to make with Cowley the "exile's return" shook his head about the destruction of individual expression, anachronistically recalling such simple forerunners of existentialism as, say, Dadaism. The existentialist may admit involvement in the Resistance Movement or paradoxically in the Communist Party, but involvement is an expedient adjustment to life. Occupational sitting in a sidewalk cafe is no more to be reproached than working for an organized cause. To the existentialist, sexual perversion, robbery, or working to get out the liberal vote cannot be excused as the determined end of a dominant mother, a background of poverty, or guilt for an early act of race discrimination: people choose to do what they tell themselves they cannot help doing. In contrast to the neo-orthodox absolutist, the existentialist has his cake and eats it too, for there is no choice that will demand penance. Even the "bad" choice to the moralist is emphatically a "free" choice to the existentialist, even if he may follow with the question of "Freedom for what?" The orthodox dualism of the reason versus the passions is replaced by the monism of the constantly choosing organism. Existentialism is in a sense naturalism with freedom added, and by some logical or verbal trick it is just as opposed to determinism, biological, psychological, economic, as is traditional Christianity.

A striking dramatization of the existentialist position is *The Stranger* by Albert Camus, who denied any formal connection with Sartre's followers. In Camus' novel the young protagonist is naïvely free of the traditional sentimentalities about mother, religion, and love, of the absolutistic and prejudicial evaluations of persons, of the conventional drive to "get ahead." I say *naïvely* because the *illusory* nature of the obligations that most people accept is later stated by the narrator, but at first *felt* by him without being articulated. Caught up in a situation in part through his characteristic non-resistance, he commits a meaningless murder. He is brought to a Kafka-like trial in which he is condemned not on the basis of the facts of the murder but for his failures to meet the traditional expectations as to remorse for his previous non-conformity. With his back figuratively to the wall of death, he redefines himself through what his existence has been rather than through a sense of the essence which his imperfect matter should reflect. He concludes that he acted as he did because he chose to and wonders "what difference could they make to me, the deaths of others, or a mother's love, or his God, or the way a man decides to live, the fate he thinks he chooses" since in the end "all alike would be condemned to die one day." These conclusions "wash" him clean and "empty" him of hope, making him paradoxically ready to start over again: "gazing up at the dark sky spangled with its signs and stars, for the first time, the first, I laid my heart open to the benign indifference of the universe." Benign indifference! the naturalists called this very indifference malignant, and the

writers of tragedy called it a kind of harmony in which
man had his place, however petty. The resignation to
one's identity, the acceptance of the recollected moments of life and the inevitability of death, that Camus
and the formal existentialists profess, is close to the
final position of the tragic hero, say, Lord Jim or
Hemingway's old man in his last novel. There is of
course the all-important difference that aloneness not
oneness, agony not hope, finality not immortality make
up the mode which is faced with equanimity.

   If the tragic hero is Christ-like in the persistence of
his faith, the admission of his follies, and the dignified
transcendence of his physical defeat, the existentialist
hero is just the opposite in his denial of commitment, his
freedom from remorse, and the almost arrogant certainty
that death is an end. The magistrate of the prison in
which Camus' hero ends up, addresses him in "a friendly
tone" as "Mr. Antichrist," but he is not entirely joking.
He has literally placed a crucifix in front of Meursault
and demanded confession and verbal penance, but all
that Meursault can muster is "a kind of vexation" rather
than the anticipated "regret." In fact, throughout the
book Meursault is the antagonist to a number of
would-be saviors whom he refuses to acknowledge. The
first of these is his mother, whose funeral he attends
in the initial scene of the book. Her coffin, in a room
bathed in deep white light, is attended by twelve persons, including the keeper and himself. He is of course
the Judas to the body in that he does not evidence the
traditional homage of son to parent. He feels incidentally
that the others present "had come to sit in judgment on
me" and senses their particular surprise at his showing no
desire to see his mother's body. Implicitly, one must

believe in a God before he can "see" him, and conversely Meursault is condemned as failing morally for not even *wanting* to see the mother, his first potential savior.

The next savior for Meursault's Judas is perhaps Perez, the mother's friend who gradually falls out of sight as Meursault and others accompany the body to the church on an oppressive walk suggesting more a descent into the abyss of hell than an ascent to the gates of heaven. If Perez, a kind of substitute father-figure, is an inept savior, Marie, with whom Meursault's relationship is singularly physical, is a deficient one. She drives even farther away the mother whom he has betrayed, but Marie is surrounded by none of the white light in which the mother's body lay: she is only the earthly part of man's dualistic nature. Raymond the pimp, who insists on friendship with Meursault, is almost melodramatically a mock-savior who perverts and complicates love, cringes before authority, and indirectly leads Meursault to his downfall in the murder of the Arab. We have already mentioned the magistrate who offers the crucifix to Meursault, the "Antichrist." Even the lawyers, like two gods, good and/or bad, fight over the prisoner's "soul," which they frequently mention as such. At the trial innumerable witnesses try to save him, only to hurt him instead. The final inadequate savior is fittingly a priest, who infuriates Meursault with insisting that in the few moments of life he has left, he "waste" them thinking of God. Meursault's knowledge that man is alone, hopeless, free of obligation to various saviors, but free too to choose the existence that precedes death which in turn chooses all men, is, he contends, a greater certainty than the priest's faith. The realization that he has chosen his existence eliminates the need for a scapegoat to bear his burdens, however heavy they may seem to the orthodox thinker.

Meursault as an Antichrist recalls Faulkner's Joe Christmas as the inverted Christ who recurrently denies a number of women who want to sustain him. The eating motif which Faulkner employs several times to illustrate Christmas' refusal to assume the Christ function through the acceptance of offered communions is used similarly by Camus. Here and there in *The Stranger* occur incompleted meals compatible with the varied deficiencies of the persons who might help Meursault. In *Light in August*, on the other hand, Christmas, who has constantly refused food and, when at last he *is* hungry, been refused it, finally eats the raw corn, almost like the god eating the god, and all but loses his substantiality; he is still hungry, we are told, but no longer hungry for *food*. In *The Grapes of Wrath* Casy says that man's sharing of food even when he doesn't have enough for himself is "bigger" than any individual man. The "grapes of wrath" are trod when surplus food that hungry men need is not shared, but destroyed in an attempt to maintain an economy of scarcity. The "bread and wine" of Silone's novel contain ceremonial communion, the natural communion of individuals, the communion of an entire society based on love instead of competition and exploitation. We shall presently see that Hemingway's old man has a last supper prepared for him almost ritualistically by his boy-disciple before the climactic fight with the big fish, and even while he is having the significant struggle of his life, he eats the raw fish, again like eating the god, not because he is literally hungry—like Christmas, he gets *beyond* that—but because he knows that he must eat if he is to endure the struggle. Camus' Antichrist who discovers the freedom of aloneness needs no communion.

The title of Camus' book may suggest, as one critic has pointed out, that Meursault remains throughout the novel a stranger to life as it is traditionally lived. On the other hand I think of the popular designation of Dionysus as the stranger god who is at first unrecognized on his annual return to Greece, and of the number of times that Christ is denied even by his closest followers. The savior gods usually come from outside the social unit they are to save through eventually serving as the sacrificed scapegoat. Lord Jim, Christmas, Mrs. Moore, Casy are all alien to Patusan, the Burden place, India, and California, their respective spheres of operation. These figures are strangers to life in a richly ambiguous sense of the word: they are human beings, but if they achieve their god functions they are superhuman. Meursault, as the existentialist protagonist, attains his freedom from the responsibilities and demands of life without, we must remember, transcending the moments which have made up his particular life. He is a stranger to life, yes, but with the existentialist elimination of essence, not at all in a dualistic sense. In this way too he seems truly an Antichrist.

There is a meaningful bit of irony in that the Antichrist, who is condemned as such, is dramatically placed in the position of serving the function of the Christ figure. All during the trial Meursault is accused of the sins of which every man is potentially guilty. He foresees that the people will greet him at his execution "with howls of execration." They will make of him a kind of scapegoat as if *he* were responsible for the absurdity of life that they all live and the oblivion of death that they must all face.

In the middle of the nineteenth century Turgenev's protagonist Bazarov of *Fathers and Sons* tried so hard to be a nihilist and died Christ-like in the performance of service to others. Meursault in his recognition and admission of his own nature achieves a kind of transcendence of which his many judges in the world are incapable until they face the crisis that will make them judge themselves. The true Antichrists may be in the last analysis those who presume to play the role of Judge of Man rather than those who are resigned to standing before the Bar of Justice.

BIBLIOGRAPHICAL NOTE:

EXISTENTIALISM AND LITERATURE

Twentieth-century existentialism, like nineteenth-century romanticism, has become such an inclusive word that any statement of its implications can be refuted by a dichotomous statement. Walter Kauffmann in his *Existentialism from Dostoyevsky to Sartre* (New York, 1958) traces both the development and the variations of literary existentialism. Sartre's famous speech on *Existentialism* (translated by Bernard Frechtman, New York, 1947) is still the Bible for and best guide to the literary existentialists. The interpretations of Camus are as rich and various as those of existentialism generally, a position toward which Camus expressed recurrently an ambivalent attitude. In the years just before his lamentable death, several interesting discussions of Camus had appeared: e.g., Germaine Brée's *Camus* (New Brunswick, N. J., 1959); John Cruickshank's *Albert Camus and the Literature of Revolt* (London, 1959); and Philip Thody's *Albert Camus: A Study of His Work* (London, 1958). Camus himself made a telling comment on *The Stranger* in the preface written for a 1955 edition of the novel and translated by Vernon Hall, Jr., for *The Nation*, November 16, 1957:

So for me, Meursault is not a mere drifter but a poor, naked human being, in love with that sun that casts no shadows. He is far from being completely without sensibility; a profound passion, though a tacit one, moves him—a passion for the absolute and for the truth. The truth at stake is as yet only negative, the truth of being and feeling. But without this truth, no conquest over oneself and over the world will ever be possible.

It would not, then, be much of an error to read *The Stranger* as the story of a man who, without any heroic posturizing, is willing to die for the truth. Once, paradoxically again, I said that I had tried to symbolize in my character the only Christ of which we are worthy. After my explanation, it should be clear that I said it without any attempt to blaspheme and with but that slightly ironic affection an artist has the right to feel for characters he has created.

XIII

Christ As The Old Champion:

HEMINGWAY'S
The Old Man and the Sea

THAT traditional tragic awareness is once again a possibility for writers is illustrated in a negative, mock sense in the individualistic rationale of existentialism and in a positive, serious sense in what I have called neo-orthodoxy. *The Stranger* I have considered as an example of existentialism. Hemingway's *The Old Man and the Sea* I should like to mention as an example of neo-orthodoxy.

Hemingway was very proud of this book, and he had a right to be, for not only has it been a best-seller but it has also received the critical plaudits of the Pulitzer and the Nobel Prize committees. Commenting on it, he said that he used to write "in arithmetic," but now he is writing "in calculus"; but there may be some question as to whether conscious arithmetic is not often unconscious calculus. In any case, back in the arithmetic days, Hemingway looked forward to the time when the calculus would be a possibility. Nick, the protagonist in many of the first forty-nine stories, is at this expectant stage in his journey of learning in "Big Two-Hearted River: Part I."

He has been wounded, presumably in the war literally and in his emotional development symbolically; he returns to his homeland as if seeking a kind of wondrous cure in uncorrupted nature or solace in the comfortable womb. But much of his homeland has been burned out, and the rituals of youth that he goes through do not cure his fatigue or heal his wound. He somehow gives up whatever miraculous hope of rebirth he has had and accepts for the moment things as they are. In the river in which he fished as a young boy before the war and the wound, he has pursued a great fish, which escapes him and disappears in the swamp.

Nick did not want to go in there now. He felt a reaction against deep wading with the water deepening up under his armpits, to hook big trout in places impossible to land them. In the swamp the banks were bare, the big cedars came together overhead, the sun did not come through, except in patches; in the fast deep water, in the half light, the fishing would be tragic. In the swamp, fishing was a tragic adventure. Nick did not want it. He did not want to go down the stream any further today.

Nick is not yet ready for tragedy, and implicitly Hemingway was not ready for it.

The early books are repeatedly statements of its impossibility. Be brave, gentle, in love, and you get kicked in the teeth, warns Lieutenant Henry in *A Farewell to Arms*, instead of emphasizing the individual integrity that moral and emotional attachment may bring over and beyond physical hurt. By the time Hemingway wrote *The Old Man and the Sea*, he had had the fine apprenticeship of dramatizing sacrifice *in* and *for* all mankind, as in *For Whom the Bell Tolls*. But in contrast to *The Grapes of Wrath* and in partial contrast to *Bread and Wine*, *The*

Old Man and the Sea is very consciously a tragedy in individual rather than in social terms. In Hemingway's story a man does go too far literally in the pursuit of the great marlin, and he goes too far because he has chosen to: "His [the fish's] choice had been to stay in the deep dark water far out beyond all snares and traps and treacheries. My choice was to go there to find him beyond all people. Beyond all people in the world. Now we are joined together and have been since noon. No one to help either of us." All of the elements of tragedy are contained in this bit of introspection: an excess that is nobody's or no thing's fault but one's own choice; a realization of a physical mistake that is nevertheless an example of moral freedom on the part of the excessive man even while he is passionately involved in his excess; an identification with the very thing which he is conventionally fighting; a kind of mature resignation to this vast thing rather than a juvenile spitting at it. The essence of classical tragedy is pointed out in detail after detail dramatizing moral victory out of the physical defeats of personal mutilation, loss of security, and lack of recognition by, say, tourists who can't tell a marlin from a shark. Toward the end of his struggle the old man expresses direct acceptance of the fish as a male life principle in the sea, a female life principle, in a way that reveals a harmony and oneness with the elements of nature and the universe in which and with which he has been struggling. It is as if his final struggle has led to the kind of wisdom that an Oedipus, for example, reaches only through protracted experience and struggling.

A pattern related to the conscious one of the classical tragic mode and structure is the even more conscious one of the old champion and the new champion.

This is developed in a number of specific ways. The apprenticeship of the attendant boy is perhaps the chief one. He has learned from the old man, attended him as a kind of devotee or disciple of a god, performing rituals of food, dress, and shelter. But alas, when the old man is at the height of his tragic climax, the boy is elsewhere, and the old man, the tutor, expresses constant need for the young boy, the student. The old man recalls when he himself was the young champion defeating by strength of hand the old champion, the Negro on the coast of Africa, in a contest that drew blood from both the defeated one and himself, ironically weakening his own, the new champion's, hand for some contest in the future. The weakened hand he treats implicitly as his Achilles' heel and relates specifically to the bone spur of Joe DiMaggio, who, like the African Negro, is "a fine man and a great athlete" even in the end of his career as champion. And at the beginning and end of the story the old man dreams of the golden lions in the African sun, which had once been a part of his young, strong experience, but is now only a memory. When the old man lies with his hands mutilated, tired, perhaps sick, perhaps near death, the boy again feeds him and dresses him and pays him homage. The spear of the fish the old man passes to the boy, symbolizing in a kind of double phallic symbol the mutability of virility and the immortality of continuity. Intentionally or not, the imagery recalls the innumerable myths of the sun gods who, in waxing, wane, only to be replaced by other sun gods who will wax and wane, wax and wane, and so on for eternity.

Both the artistic concept of tragedy, in which man gains dignity through suffering, and the mythic structure of the old champion, at his physical end and in a way his spiritual beginning, of course include the Christ pattern. Hemingway's imagery is a broader anthropological imagery, but several references make clear that he utilizes Christ as one symbol among symbols. Chief among these are the mutilated hands, the ambivalent images of blood, the explicit statements of suffering, the carrying of the mast on his shoulders from the boat to his final rest, when he "slept face down . . . with his arms out straight and the palms of his hands out." How different from the earlier Hemingway who preached the danger of involvement and the advisability of building a shell against natural emotion. Now in effect he says, Greek-like, that suffering brings wisdom and, Christian-like, that suffering leads to moral victory.

Hemingway's old man, who takes complete responsibility for his excesses and in so doing transcends his physical defeat, is in contrast to the socially conscious Christ-archetype of the proletarian novel with its emphasis on the brotherhood of man. If any direction can be recognized in the themes of American literature since the 'thirties, it is this growing distrust of the group and the tendency to take blame for one's failures and praise for one's potentialities. This attitude is understandable as a part of the post-war, cold-war climate of exhaustion with world struggle, disappointment with Russia as a socialist ideal, and anti-New-Dealism and McCarthyism at home. It is as if the intellectuals, wearying of the denial of social hope by the repeated turn of events and accepting the inevitability of physical defeat, have turned to highly individualistic and introspective solutions. Disillusioned with the possibility of solving problems at the social level, many writers and thinkers and spokesmen in a variety of fields of endeavor have somehow made the jump of faith to transcendental and supernatural answers.

Hemingway was not alone. Faulkner and Steinbeck, to mention two of the writers we have discussed, both moved on to consider the problems of sin, penance, and absolution in *Requiem for a Nun* and *East of Eden* respectively, and even before that they were handling consciously the structure and themes of classical tragedy in, say, *Absalom, Absalom!* and *The Pearl.* Faulkner's more recent *A Fable,* for example, treated without subtlety, and with heavy seriousness for the most part, the traditional drama of institutional Christianity, which is decried in *Light in August* as leaving out love, the essential and unique saving grace.

This more or less neo-orthodoxy seems particularly characteristic of the older, established writers—Hemingway, Faulkner, Steinbeck, Eliot, Auden—rather than of the young novelists of "promise." Perhaps here there is something akin to the impossibility of Oedipus' learning wisdom through suffering until, to put it redundantly, he has suffered. The very fact of age, of which the writers who were young in the 'twenties would be very much aware, makes the mature man conceive of tragedy, for if he doesn't realize that death is inevitable, then he becomes in middle or old age a sputtering adolescent like an elderly man wearing clothes too young for him. Somehow the universal theme must, in the last analysis, be the answer to the Sphinx's questions which Oedipus, young, strong, smart, can give intellectually, but which he cannot understand emotionally until he is old, bent, humble. The answer "Man" to the question of what first moves on four legs, then two, then three, is richly implicit, for here is the statement of the certainty of

flux. How can youth after all understand that he too is
born to die—that is, after he has questioned his father's
mores, jeered at old age, replaced the father totally,
thumped his chest with confidence, become altogether
the cock of the walk?

In the tragic learning of the inevitability of one's
own physical catastrophe and the subsequent adjustment
to spiritual transcendence is the meeting ground for all
critical approaches. The mythic theme concerns the old
champion replaced by the new champion who will become the old champion. The religious theme: literal
birth, literal death, and spiritual rebirth. The tragic
theme: the proud man who meets his fall and learns
humility, a higher wisdom than pride. The biological
theme: man born, man aged, man having reproduced the
son who will continue him. The psychological theme:
the son who fights the authority of the father only to
become a father whose son ungratefully fights his
authority. The socio-economic theme: the thesis which
is forced by the antithesis into a synthesis, which is
then the new thesis to be faced with a new antithesis.
The domestic theme: the modern anxiety of every company president, conservative politician, scholarly professor, well-known writer threatened by every imaginative young vice president, liberal campaigner, new critic,
experimental artist.

In that embarrassingly naked book, *Across the
River and into the Trees,* Hemingway expressed all of
the sense of age in the pathetic way of a man trying
desperately to be young. The young critics jeered: after
all, they said, he is not the writer he's cracked up to be.
But whether he was trying to or not, Hemingway wrote
one of the truly sad books of our time, conveying remark-

ably how shocking it is to see the bald spot in the back of one's head for the first time. Almost the predictable adjustment was *The Old Man and the Sea,* with the catharsis of tragedy that doesn't make physical change matter anyway. In these terms life is death and death is life. The orthodox funeral sermon which makes this emphasis is dichotomous with Casy's insistence that living is holy, "and that's what matters."

The biological, the psychological, and the social changes of the individual, the patterns of history as seen by everyone from Sir Walter Raleigh to Spengler to Toynbee, the cycle of the seasons, create the dramatic context for the Christ-archetype. The sociologist might even contend that the religious and tragic literature comes at the end of cultures: it is then that men create the great figures of continuation in spite of it all— Krishna, Dionysus, Christ, and the Others.

In *A Farewell to Arms,* back in the year of *The Modern Temper,* Lieutenant Henry was reminded by the peasants and the very old Italian diplomat Count Greffi that only the defeated peoples win wars, a lesson that Henry never really understands, for Hemingway's protagonists were not yet ready for "a tragic adventure." Recall that the same elderly gentleman tells Henry that when other members of his family became old, they became religious, but that he has waited for faith to come, still in vain. This worldly, noble, mannered old man, drinking fine cold wine, confirms Krutch's contention in 1929 of the intellectual articulation of tragedy, but the emotional incomprehension of it. Hemingway's last old man, a poor fisherman, wears his sense of tragedy like a newly acquired cloak.

BIBLIOGRAPHICAL NOTE:

A COMPENDIUM OF APPROACHES

The critical responses to Hemingway's *The Old Man and the Sea* ranged from the extravagantly admiring to the exaggeratedly disdainful. Carlos Baker wrote in *The Saturday Review* (September 6, 1952): "'The Old Man and the Sea' is a great short novel, told with consummate artistry and destined to become a classic in its kind. It is a good kind of present for a man to give the world on or about his fifty-third birthday." And in the same month Seymour Krim wrote in *Commonweal* (September 19, 1952): "Hemingway has already done the significant part of his life's work. . . . He is, by our living needs and standards, a true, brilliant, but very limited artist, and I believe that we have gotten all we can from him now." It was at least reassuring that after Hemingway's death, critics were inspired to judge the total body of his work rather than to say readily: the man is done for, he has not developed, we were wrong in the first place, as they said when both *Across the River and into the Trees* and *The Old Man and the Sea* appeared. Now some of them, like Krim, might say in their eulogies: we were wrong in the second place.

A fine discussion of established critical approaches and a suggestion of a fruitful one of his own is Stanley Edgar Hyman's *The Armed Vision: A Study in the Methods of Modern Literary Criticism* (New York, 1948). Mr. Hyman has since directed his attention strikingly to myth-and-literature and become one of the richest definers of the relationship.

XIV

The End Is The Beginning . . .

A FEW years ago an article in the Sunday *Magazine* of the New York *Times* distinguished between the lost generation of the 1920's, which was shocked to find itself pushed into an abyss, and the beat generation of the 1940's and 1950's, which, already in the abyss, was struggling to climb out. Kenneth Burke talks of literature as varieties of "strategies of adjustment," and the novels we have discussed may very well be distinguished from each other as adjustments to the abyss. The metaphor is a rather discouraging one, for no difference of material plight is recognized. But it is pertinent, for after all who except an ostrich can deny an intellectual climate of opinion about the observable and predictable nature of man in a particular kind of universe? E. M. Forster in his fine statement "What I Believe" says that we cannot deny the inevitability of force in the cycles of history, but he objects equally to those who worship force and those who declare its non-existence. His concern is how to live in spite of it, and though his conclusions are irrelevant to our purposes here, he believes that man can

and does creatively snatch the interims when force is
latent instead of dominant. Force, it can be assumed, is
only one implication of the abyss, which can include,
besides, historical determinism, man's biological and
psychological plight, and other naturalistic accoutrements. About five years ago I heard W. H. Auden dis-
tinguish between natural man who is trapped and historical man who is free, a distinction which might be
described as his attempt to climb out of the abyss. Engels,
who equated freedom with "the recognition of necessity," would have accused Auden of trying to have his
cake and eat it too, and even to the early Auden, a dichotomy between natural and historical was false. Indeed,
even the problem would have been considered illusory.
Still, in Auden's simple distinction is a springboard for all
creativity, tragedy, orthodox faith, and unorthodox existentialism, the very bases of the new freedoms which
writers have recently been trying to define.

That Christ has come constantly to symbolize man's
trap *and* man's freedom we have already pointed out
as a natural consequence of Western culture. When
there is no climate of transcendent belief, old men ready
to die wait in vain for religion, young men are fooled
by false springs, tired men seek futilely rejuvenation,
misdirected men search unsuccessfully for the East, and
yearning men call the god but he does not come. The
very religious and mythic imagery of the narratives of
bitter disappointment and disillusionment nevertheless
point out the author's strong conditioning to the rituals
of belief or at least an unconscious and natural awareness
of them. It is, again, like Catherine Barkley who recalls
being taught that everything had an explanation. Shock
at being in the abyss can be expressed in anger, bitter-

ness, studied detachment, cynicism, and subtle irony, and it can be dramatized in nostalgia for and mockery of such deifications of values as Christ.

A struggle to climb out of the abyss, or rather somehow to rise above one's inevitable plight in it, takes the form dramatically of Jung's "modern man in search of a soul"—and in Western literature, especially, of an approach to a godhead personified in some facet of Christ. This personification of ideals must be by the very nature of fiction a symbol of dualism, who establishes verisimilitude in that he walks, talks, eats as a man but demands symbolic reading in that he promises a truth beyond apparent truth. His characterization simply "clothes" an ideal. Conrad in a sense was angry with those who let themselves fall into the abyss: not the "liver," but the "soul," he insisted. At one point when Lord Jim badly needed a job, he was offered work by one Chester, who had a "gold-mine" in a "guano island." Jim was, suggests Marlow, offended. " 'Takes it to heart?' he [Chester] asked scornfully. 'Very much,' I [Marlow] said. 'Then he's no good,' he opined. 'What's all the to-do about? A bit of ass's skin. That never made a man. You must see things exactly as they are—' " "Yes," Conrad has Marlow answer ironically, "you see things as they are," but to Conrad there was always the "something else besides." The abyss of the jungle was always there, but not as an environmental plight, rather as an innate one, and the potentiality of freedom, growing too out of an innate capacity, was ever present. Conrad could hang over the edge by his toes with his insistence on innateness, but he *felt* and he was persistent and that was that. He had after all a chronological advantage over the later writers who had been taught formally and implicitly that they were trapped, caught, surrounded, and that their only adjustment was to articulate their plight and be resigned to it, not with tragic dignity but with self-pity for themselves and pathos for others. Conrad was fighting a *current* battle: he had, like Catherine, been taught otherwise, and he had the advantage of any incumbent—though parties in office do eventually change.

Working their way emotionally, intellectually, artistically to Conrad's advantage from the disadvantageous education of the late nineteenth and experience of the early twentieth centuries, writers who have grown up, as it were, in the pit have arrived at a variety of strategies for transcending it. These need hardly be repeated: primitive Christianity which was more love than self-flagellation, social Christianity which finds love of mankind adequate even if love of God is elusive, an individualistic yet socially-conscious Christianity which talks of mass individual "changes of heart" rather than of group action, a neo-orthodoxy which accepts a doctrine of necessary suffering as a step to transcendent love and moral victory. If one dares mention it in the same breath, a doctrine of non-essential existentialism must fall psychologically in the last category, because even without a conscious belief in spiritual order its chief emphasis is individual responsibility, individual agony, and individual freedom. There is the irony of Camus, for example, talking of Antichrists who have the same attributes of the highly traditional Christ who *chooses* crucifixion and thereby *gains* freedom. Christ and the other spring-god archetypes are in effect an easy verbal way out. After all, to know that spring follows winter, that people do live on, that the depraved flesh leads to innocent birth, one doesn't need formal training or the techniques of logic: one simply needs to live and he *knows* in the truly comprehensive way that includes *feels* as well. Christ in the Western culture has become the other half of the metaphor that the Symbolists employed so assiduously. To argue about his implications as, say, Steinbeck as against Silone as against Faulkner as against Hemingway employs them, is to cause schisms, to create sects, but nevertheless there he is in one related facet or another as the *dramatic* guide to the way out of the abyss.

The great religions, all of which revolve around some form of the Christ-archetype, formulate themselves, we have suggested, when persons for one reason or another become strikingly aware of the end of manners and/or basic substructures. Can this possibly mean that the religious-mythic emphasis of recent literature is a warning that we are living in a vastly significant period of transition and, furthermore, a warning against smugness? In this sense, Faulkner's advantage was his chronological relationship to the feudal South, now all but dead: he simply had the compulsion to use earlier than his industrially-environmented colleagues a universal religious imagery, which is communicated to his Western readers primarily by his cluster of Christ references.

One other point remains to be made. I have suggested that at some time or other in their works all writers talk directly about the problems of their art; and it can easily be argued from the Freudian or almost any point of view that all writers are primarily concerned with the problem of the artist in society. All fiction, said such diverse writers as Thomas Wolfe and Thomas Mann, is autobiographical in the most inclusive sense of the word. Reconsider Conrad insisting on the "something else besides" and writing his circumlocutious prose, Steinbeck working Casy through his progress from amoral naturalism to social belief, Faulkner making a character say that one can understand a person if he only "reads" his name in time. These are direct discussions of techniques by the authors, but they are also direct references to dominating themes. Too, a writer *has* to like his central character, to demand sympathy for him even if he is as hectically "evil" as Christmas, *has* to identify himself with his protagonist and/or his central intelligence.

Seeing Christ as the artist in society, loving, hostile to materialism, articulate, misunderstood, mistreated, requires no remarkable sense of similitude in dissimilitude. He may be the ideal sought in vain—and this strategy results in vehement and mocking social criticism—or he may be the ideal approached as one traces one's own development. But the artist is, as Wordsworth insists, a man, and after all more than a man from the artist's own point of view, however narcissistic or humble. Too, whatever happens to the artist in his lifetime, in Christ as a symbol is the assurance of immortality. Milton, Shelley, Tennyson, Arnold in their great elegies all adjusted to the early deaths of articulate young men, with whom they could readily identify themselves, by disclaiming any interest in worldly fame and replacing it with belief in an otherworldly heaven. Once more Christ is *the* fruitful Western example of continuation in spite of physical disappointment. And who doesn't wish for a strategy to transcend his immeasurable measurable problems?

This desire after all doesn't make the artist very

different from the millworker, housewife, and metropolitan executive. Every man's problem is the heads or tails of Christ's coin. Using Christ as a central or recurrent symbol, the artist then may express himself, employ a universal frame of reference, handle the current climate, and speak to every reader in every time. Whether or not they effect changes in the environment, the strategies revolving around Christ as a dramatic symbol are infinite in their aesthetic wisdom. Their appeal to the reader is eternal.

BIBLIOGRAPHICAL NOTE:

IN ADDITION TO THE GREAT ONES

The New York *Times* essay on "The Beat Generation" (*Magazine*, November 16, 1952) was by Clellon Holmes, a friend and critic of Jack Kerouac. Holmes' best known works are *Go*, a highly autobiographical novel having as easily identifiable characters himself, the poet Alan Ginsberg, and Kerouac, and *The Horn*, a wonderfully structured and well-written novel about a jazzman. Holmes' *Go* is Kerouac's *On the Road* from a different point of view—and though it is more controlled, it is a less vigorous and less significant piece of work. The beat novels and poems as they have developed frequently have as their center *wise fools*, who are somehow so far beyond the pale of the society to which they in effect preach that they are never in danger of martyrdom. Again, it is as if the Oriental serenity of Zen Buddhism makes completely absurd the penitential and painful sacrifice at the center of Christianity's drama. The sound of one hand clapping may be contrasted to the agonies on and around the cross. An effective juxtaposition of the two occurs in Tennessee Williams' latest play, *The Night of the Iguana*, when the old-maid artist in an Oriental kimona prepares tea next to the defrocked priest tied and writhing in a hammock. Alan Watts' *Beat Zen, Square Zen, and Zen* (San Francisco, 1959) might be read along with Kerouac's *The Dharma Bums*. "Lost and Hollow, Beat and Angry: The Significant

Gestures of Two Generations," a speech which I gave at the Portland
State Festival of Contemporary Arts in 1959 (printed later in the
Ball State *Forum*, Winter, 1960-1961), pays attention to the Christ
pattern of the beat writers:

But, you say, if their objections to tne brutality of war, the un-
scrupulousness of business, the hypocrisy of religion, the falseness of
learning are so strong, what are they doing about it? Unlike the
writers of the 'thirties who had—indeed as all serious writers do—
the same enemies, the beat writers suspect group action for social
ends as much as they do the system which needs attention. Turn-the-
other-cheek, the individual vow-of-poverty, the Love of Man-for-
Man (man-for-man, man-for-woman, woman-for-woman) are highly
respectable solutions on paper in the Western world with its Judaeo-
Christian icing, but highly individualistic ones. In a peculiar sense the
beat group sees itself as monks denying the world: the vow of poverty, the vow of chastity (sex is holy!), the vow of obedience (to
the cult, even in the religious garb worn, a garb highly reminiscent
of the Master: beard and sandals). The inefficacy of the modern disciple is emphasized in his need for such artificial aids as marijuana
and heroin to help him achieve his mystical kick. The sort of dirty-
pastoral escape into the rundown slums of mock-Venice-by-the-sea
is too close in time for romanticization into a poor and holy rabble,
though this is precisely how the groups see themselves. *Beat* has
moved from *beaten* (the pathos of man undone by a world he never
made), to *downbeat* (free of the rat-race by choice), to *beatific*
(capable of transcending the illusions of the world which caused
them to suffer).

The same speech, incidentally, commented on the grail pattern of
the angry ones, highly pertinent to the Christ pattern:

Jimmy Porter's wife Alison [in *Look Back in Anger*], reminding us
of the epithet "holy barbarians" which Lawrence Lipton in his book
of that title applies to the beat artists, calls her husband a "spiritual
barbarian" who "threw down the gauntlet" at her and changed her
"happy, uncomplicated life"—or Osborne suggests, her sterile life
though she didn't recognize its sterility.
One thinks again of the archetypal pattern of the dead land
which the life-giving figure, alien to the setting, rejuvenates through
his strength and purity and sometimes capacity for suffering. . . .
Think too of such a dramatist as Tennessee Williams, so fond of
potent young men and of decadent women who might be rejuve-
nated, and of his disciple William Inge, who in *Picnic* sends a kind
of American sungod—almost a literal picaro—into an inhibited mid-
dleclass town. A universal pattern, yes, but one of which contemporary writers are very much aware.

Kenneth Burke's essay on literature as "strategies of adjustment" is the title essay of *The Philosophy of Literary Form* (Baton Rouge, 1941). Forster's "What I Believe" was included in a collection of personal statements published in 1939. Auden's speech I heard on a lecture series at Bethany College, Bethany, West Virginia, but it suggests much of what he has to say in his long poem *Age of Anxiety*. Holmes' pioneering essay on "The Beat Generation" was extended and answered in a speech given by Jack Kerouac at Brandeis University, which was reprinted, of all places, in *Playboy* in 1959.

The names Kerouac, Osborne, and Williams have occurred above. Add Salinger, and one has perhaps the most striking names among recent English and American voices. Certainly such writers as Nathanael West (particularly his *A Cool Million* and *Miss Lonelyhearts*) and Salinger (all of him: *The Catcher in the Rye, Nine Stories,* and *Frannie and Zooey*) might be fruitfully considered in a study such as mine. Salinger is a good writer certainly, but whether he is a great writer, whether he is in "the big league" as Hemingway would have said, will have ultimately something to do with quantity as well as quality. But so far, he is fine, and so far too, he is, one might say, primarily concerned with how one can be Christ in our time *and* live.

A Bibliographical Index